THE STORY OF
THE VICTORIA LINE

WALTHAMSTOW CENTRAL British Rail

BLACKHORSE ROAD British Rail

TOTTENHAM HALE British Rail

SEVEN SISTERS British Rail

FINSBURY PARK Piccadilly Line. British Rail

HIGHBURY AND ISLINGTON Northern Line. British Rail

KING'S CROSS / ST. PANCRAS Northern, Met., Circle & Piccadilly Lines. British Rail

EUSTON Northern Line. British Rail

WARREN STREET Northern Line

OXFORD CIRCUS Central & Bakerloo Lines

GREEN PARK Piccadilly Line

VICTORIA District & Circle Lines. British Rail

PIMLICO

VAUXHALL British Rail

STOCKWELL Northern Line

BRIXTON British Rail

RIVER THAMES

VICTORIA LINE Sketch map showing rail interchange facilities.

THE STORY OF
The Victoria Line

BY JOHN R. DAY

M.C.I.T., ASSOC.I.R.S.E.

LONDON TRANSPORT

© London Transport
first published 1969
revised edition 1970
reprinted 1971
second revised edition 1972

SBN. 85329 020 2

CONTENTS

1 How it all began

ON 22 JUNE 1907, David Lloyd George opened the Charing Cross, Euston & Hampstead Railway, advertised widely as the 'Last Link' in the London Tube Railway network. Confident as the tone of this announcement was, it is improbable that at that time anyone could have realized that it would be 62 years before the next cross-London line would be in service.

It was not that the tube railway system stood still for all these years—there was great expansion, especially to the north and west, and even new links in inner London, but none of these formed a new route across the centre.

It is plain that a system of Underground railways in which each line was conceived at a different time, for a different purpose, and quite independently of all the others, must leave much to be desired when it comes to taking the shortest distance between two points and making the easiest possible interhcange between one line and another. This thought was in the minds of many concerned with London's transport, and although much was done by London Transport and its predecessors to make interchange as easy as possible through underground subways, the task was difficult, expensive, and the results not always very convenient when completed.

One great opportunity for broad-scale planning came when in 1933 the newly formed London Passenger Transport Board (LPTB) took over all London's Underground railways—except the Waterloo & City, which still belongs to British Railways—and could look at the problems with a single mind. With the assistance of the Government, the LPTB, the London & North Eastern Railway, and the Great Western Railway launched the 1935–40 New Works programme, or £40 million plan, which brought great improvements to services in the London dormitory areas, resulted in a major expansion of the Underground, and took tube trains out on to former LNER and GWR tracks.* This plan, however, apart from some station works, did not affect central London. The work was begun and much of it was completed either before or during the early months of the war, but some had to be suspended and completed after the end of hostilities. In the changed circumstances, some of the plan was cancelled, or carried out later with modifications.

It was the war which gave the first chance of an overall view of London as a place where people lived, worked, played, shopped, and performed all the multifarious activities which make up human life. A massive survey, the County of London Plan, was prepared by J. H. Forshaw, architect to the London County Council, and Professor Sir Patrick Abercrombie: it appeared in 1943 and was followed the next year by Sir Patrick's Greater London Plan. One of the points made by the planners was that railway works and installations in London were often ugly and stood in the way of good planning. Yet they understood very well how important the railways were in enabling the capital to function.

The solution they advocated, in broad terms, was to get as many railway facilities as possible under the ground, including some of the termini, and to build full-scale tube tunnels capable of taking main-line size suburban stock and giving connections between main-line termini. They also placed importance on the separation of main-line and suburban trains. Where possible, their new tube tunnels were to connect with the existing Underground lines. The northern part of the Circle Line was earmarked as a route for freight trains—a role not strange to that section of it, between King's Cross and Moorgate, which carries British Railways passenger trains on two extra tracks known as the 'Widened Lines'.

As might have been expected, and as the planners themselves admitted, the plans proposed for railways

*Details of the 1935–40 Works Programme, and the history of all the London Underground lines, will be found in *The Story of London's Underground*, uniform with this volume.

were not always practical when it came to running the trains on which so many depended—and still depend—for their daily transport into and out of London. It was suggested, by the planners, that a special investigating committee should be set up to examine the technical and operational aspects of the railway proposals of the County of London Plan. Such a committee, the Railway (London Plan) Committee, was set up by Lord Leathers, Minister of War Transport, on 22 February 1944 under the chairmanship of Professor Sir Charles Inglis.

The Committee submitted an interim report to the Minister in January 1945 and a final report on 21 January 1946. Although appreciating the reasoning behind the railway proposals put forward in the County of London Plan, they found themselves, generally, unable to agree with any of them except a proposal for a short north–south connecting tunnel link in central London between Snow Hill (near Farringdon) and Loughborough Junction (Brixton) to replace an existing viaduct.

The Committee did put forward alternative proposals of its own, and one of these, 'Route 8', as it was called in the report, is of particular interest. It was designed to link the electrified Southern Railway with the L N E R, the suburban services of which, the Committee stated, needed to be electrified. Route 8 was to be of main-line train size and to link East Croydon with Finsbury Park. There would be intermediate stations at Brixton, Stockwell, Vauxhall, Victoria, Hyde Park Corner, Bond Street, Euston, and King's Cross—not dissimilar from the present Victoria Line route between Brixton and Finsbury Park, except that it would have run farther to the West after leaving Victoria, calling at Hyde Park Corner instead of Green Park and Bond Street instead of Oxford Circus.

The reasons given for recommending various new lines included some relevant to Route 8 which could be used almost unchanged for building the Victoria Line today. They included the lack of a direct railway connection between Victoria, Mayfair, and Oxford Street to meet the needs of the heavy traffic using the District

Line from Victoria to Charing Cross and changing there
to reach the West End, the circuitous nature of the rail
connection between Victoria and Euston and King's
Cross, and the need to relieve the heavily used northern
section of the Piccadilly Line. Route 8 was placed in the
first priority group.

The Committee's report went to Alfred Barnes, who
had succeeded Lord Leathers as Minister of War
Transport, on 21 January 1946. It was followed on
3 March 1948 by a further report dealing with certain
railway terminals north of the Thames and with freight
traffic and distribution. In the meantime, on 1 January
1948, the British Transport Commission had assumed
ownership, among other things, of the main-line railways and the railways of the London Passenger Transport Board. As its duties included responsibility for the
co-ordination and integration of transport, the Minister
of Transport agreed that it should have the opportunity
of reviewing the earlier railway proposals for London
and the Commission appointed a committee with Sir
Cyril Hurcomb, Chairman of the Commission, at its
head.

The Committee in turn set up a 'Working Party'
under the chairmanship of V. M. Barrington-Ward, a
Member of the Railway Executive, to carry out detailed investigations. Whereas the Railway (London
Plan) Committee had been obliged to regard the
planning objective of the removal of the main railway
bridges across the Thames (at Charing Cross, Black-
friars, and Cannon Street) as of prime importance and
had to design many of their railway proposals with the
need to provide alternatives to the bridges in mind, the
Working Party were charged with giving first importance to traffic needs. They also had access to later and
more detailed forecasts of population trends and likely
future traffic needs, and were not required to consider
freight movements except where they were related to
passenger facilities.

The report of the Working Party, with a covering
letter signifying the general agreement of the British

Transport Commission to the proposals, was sent to the Minister (Alfred Barnes) on 1 February 1949. Heading the list of proposals was a new tube railway, Route C, to run from the Tottenham/Edmonton area via Finsbury Park, King's Cross, Euston, Oxford Circus, Green Park, Victoria, Vauxhall, Stockwell, Brixton, and Streatham to East Croydon. Branch lines on the alignment of the Cambridge Road and from Seven Sisters to Walthamstow were described as 'possibly desirable'. This is Route 8 again, with changes to give better traffic objectives in the centre, including Oxford Circus, where there would be cross-platform interchange with the Bakerloo Line. The recommendation that Route C should be a 'tube' line in 12-ft. diameter tunnels instead of the 17-ft. diameter main-line rolling stock size recommended by the earlier body was mainly on the grounds of economy of construction, although improved interchange possibilities played a part.

Considering Route 8, the Working Party pointed out that it covered one of the most important in-town sections for local traffic between Victoria and King's Cross and that it ought therefore to be worked by an urban service and have limitations placed on its projections beyond the central area. The Green Park and Oxford Circus alignment was preferred to that via Hyde Park Corner and Bond Street as likely to carry heavier traffic, especially outside the peak hours. At Oxford Circus, where interchange facilities were desired, there would not have been room for a tunnel of main-line size in the below-ground labyrinth.

Apart from giving swift distribution of passengers arriving at King's Cross, St. Pancras, Euston, and Victoria main-line stations and giving important in-town connections, the northern end of the route would relieve the heavily loaded Piccadilly Line north of King's Cross. Interchange with the Eastern Region lines was also regarded as an important feature. Towards the south, interchange with the Southern Region was envisaged at Victoria, Vauxhall, Brixton, Streatham Hill, Streatham, Norbury and East Croydon.

As a matter of interest, another route (Route D) given high priority was a 'tube' line which would have been fed from the eastern end by the Enfield Town and Chingford branches of the Eastern Region (steam-worked at that time but now electrified) and have followed the general alignment of Fleet Street to the west, with stations at Liverpool Street, Bank, Ludgate Circus, Aldwych, Trafalgar Square, the Army & Navy Stores in mid-Victoria Street, and Victoria. This was a variation of the earlier report's Route 9. The Working Party also envisaged a larger-diameter tube for outer-suburban trains across the central area from north-west to south-east, likewise following the Strand–Fleet Street alignment (Route F). Read in conjunction with the Working Party's plea for a Baker Street–Bond Street–Green Park route, we can see the forerunner of the Fleet Line, the first section of which, with government and Greater London Council financial support, is now under construction.

Another route, though given low priority by the Working Party, was an extension of the Aldwych branch of the Piccadilly Line southwards under the river to Waterloo to help in the opening up of the South Bank area. This proposal is also being pursued currently by London Transport and Parliamentary powers for it were granted in 1965.

At the time of the Working Party report, the latest population figure for the London Transport area (mid-1948) was 9,689,000 and the planned ultimate was 9,414,000, or a reduction of 275,000. The latest available population figure before the alteration to London Transport's responsibilities brought about by the Transport (London) Act 1969 was 10,092,000 (mid-1969). Preliminary census reports issued in August 1971 suggest that the Central London population is gradually falling.

II Route C takes shape

IN A PAPER read on 11 February 1954, L. C. Hawkins, then a Member of the London Transport Executive, stated that the southern extension of Route C would run from Victoria to Fulham Broadway, where it would join the Wimbledon line: this was yet another variation on a possible theme. At the same time he pointed out that with the then current costs of construction and equipment the line could not be self-supporting.

Self-supporting or not, there were powerful reasons for building the new line. The Committee of Inquiry into London Transport, appointed by A. T. Lennox-Boyd, then Minister of Transport, on 28 April 1953 and generally known as the Chambers Committee after S. P. Chambers, its chairman, reported in January 1955. Paragraph 452 of the report is worth quoting in full. It said:

'Although the proposed railway may not in the near future pay its way directly we are of the opinion that the indirect advantages to London Transport and to London's economy as a whole are so important that this project should not be abandoned or postponed because on the basis of direct revenue or direct expenditure it appears to be unprofitable. We are particularly concerned with the very heavy expenditure on roads which will be necessary if London's tube railways are unable to cope with passenger traffic effectively. Expenditure on new tube railways may prove to be less costly than expenditure on roads and more effective in moving large numbers of passengers. Adequate tube railways may prove to be a more effective means of relieving traffic congestion than many more controversial and more expensive schemes which have been put forward.'

In November 1954, John Boyd-Carpenter, Minister of Transport & Civil Aviation, gave his consent to the inclusion of enabling powers for the construction of Route C in the British Transport Commission Private Bill to be introduced in the next session of Parliament. This was done to enable the working plans to be completed and put the British Transport Commission in a position to begin the work if and when a decision to build the line was made. At about the same time, Sir John Elliot, Chairman of the London Transport Executive, was proposing that the State should guarantee the interest on the capital for building new tube railways to relieve street congestion in London.

Details of the new line included in the Bill showed that the situation had been examined realistically, and as it was obviously impossible to obtain enough money for both routes C and D, modifications had been made to Route C to compensate in some measure for this. For example, the new tube was now to run to Walthamstow, Wood Street on the Eastern Region Chingford branch (which was to have been part of Route D) and cross-platform interchange between London Transport and Eastern Region lines was to be provided on the surface. A new station at Highbury was to give cross-platform interchange with the Northern City Line, so giving a convenient route to the City—another small compensation for the delay to Route D. The proposal on the Working Party map to have a Route C station at Manor House, which would have involved diverting the Piccadilly Line away from that station, was dropped. The Victoria terminal was so planned that the line could have been continued to Fulham Broadway and Wimbledon.

Before a House of Commons Committee on 1 July 1955, A. B. B. Valentine, Member of the British Transport Commission, made the important point that the new line would benefit many thousands of people who might not even use it—it would divert many passengers from existing lines because of the direct journeys it would give between important central area points. For example, the Victoria–King's Cross journey would be direct and take only 13 minutes instead of 23 minutes by existing lines, including two changes.

On 5 December 1955, Sir John Elliot gave a paper to the Metropolitan Section of the Institute of Transport which marked the beginning of a new phase. He gave Route C a name at last—the Victoria Line (unless, as he modestly commented, someone could think of something better). Allowing for interest charges, he put the possible loss on working the line at £2,250,000 a year, but pointed out the benefits the line would bring to London travel generally, including lessened congestion on the roads if bus and car commuters turned to the new rail artery. He explained that means had to be found to pay for the construction if Parliament granted powers to construct the line (the Bill had very nearly finished its Parliamentary progress, with little opposition) and once more issued a plea for public money to build the line on the ground of 'the special and unprecedented problem of London street congestion'.

The powers were duly granted under the British Transport Commission Act, 1955, but nothing much else happened—there was no money. In December 1956, Political & Economic Planning came out with a booklet claiming that underground railways were a much better investment than motorways in areas where land value was high—as in London. They put the cost of a new underground railway at £4 million a mile and the cost of an urban motorway at £11 million. The respective carrying capacities were claimed as 39,000 an hour in one direction against 3,000 an hour in cars, or 20,000 in cars and buses, for the roadway.

Questions in Parliament in 1957 elicited from Harold Watkinson, then Minister of Transport & Civil Aviation, the fact that he had had an approach about the line from the British Transport Commission and was considering the financial problems. A large capital expenditure was needed, he explained, and there was the problem of whether it could be made to pay or would show a heavy loss. 'London Transport in 1957', the LTE's annual review, agreed that the line could not pay its way because much of the traffic would be transferred from existing services, but pointed out that it would relieve road congestion and attract some new traffic.

In the Lords, in February 1958, Lord Latham asked why, if grants were made by the Minister of Transport for new roads, they should not also be made for underground roads. The Minister could make a grant equivalent to the usual amount for new roads or service the debt incurred in building the new tube line. Lord Mancroft, Minister without Portfolio, accepted the validity of the argument that a new tube line would relieve congestion on the roads above, but said the London tubes were outside the problem he was dealing with that day (the acquisition of land for roads).

Meanwhile, technical planning of the Victoria Line was still going forward. By 1959 it was well advanced. By the end of that year boreholes had been sunk along the length of the new line to test subsoil conditions and nine of the thirteen stations had been designed. The New Works office of London Transport's Chief Civil Engineer's Department was well into the detailed planning it would continue for the next few years. The two firms of Consulting Engineers, Sir William Halcrow & Partners and Messrs. Mott, Hay and Anderson, were at work on contract drawings. Parliamentary powers were being sought for alterations to the Northern City tunnels at Highbury to give cross-platform interchange with the Victoria Line and negotiations were in progress with British Railways on the detailed design of the sub-surface stations at Euston and King's Cross.

In answer to a Parliamentary question on the extent to which building the line would relieve unemployment, Harold Watkinson, the Minister of Transport in February 1959, put the labour element in a six-year programme to build the Victoria Line and its rolling stock at 50,000 man-years. In reply to another question, a month later, he said that the British Transport Commission now put the cost of the line at £55 million and its estimated annual loss at £3 million, of which £2¼–2½ million would represent interest charges on capital. This was on the same day, 25 March, that he

also referred to his search for a successor to Sir John
Elliot who had intimated that he wished to resign. Sir
John retired on 30 June and was succeeded by A. B. B.
Valentine, who had had wide experience of London
Transport problems in previous years.

The London Travel Committee, under the chairmanship of Alexander Samuels, was set up to examine the
scope of, and the feasibility of, building the Victoria
Line and also to recommend to the Minister any
measures thought desirable for the relief of peak traffic
congestion in central London which the Committee
could not itself initiate, and its report therefore carried
considerable weight. It also had the great merit of
being an independent survey.

On 28 July 1959, the report of the London Travel
Committee—one of the things for which the Minister
was waiting before he made a decision—was completed
and placed in the Minister's hands. It recommended
the building of the Victoria Line as a useful addition to
the transport facilities of London in any circumstances.
Asked on 2 December by C. F. H. Gough, the
Member for Horsham, whether he had authorized the
BTC to proceed with the construction of the Victoria
Line, Ernest Marples, who was then Minister of
Transport, replied that he was carefully studying the
London Travel Committee's report. The report was
issued later the same month.

On 2 December 1961, London Transport announced
a major change in the plans for the alignment of the
Victoria Line in the Walthamstow area. It was now to
terminate not at the Eastern Region's Wood Street
station as originally intended but at Hoe Street station
in the centre of Walthamstow some three-quarters of a
mile on the London side of Wood Street. Interchange
with the Eastern Region electrified services to Highams
Park and Chingford would be provided at Hoe Street
instead of at Wood Street as formerly intended. This
change had been brought about by the progress of
electrification on the Eastern Region line through
Walthamstow to Chingford. The electrification was on

B

the overhead system, using high voltage alternating current, and major alterations would have been needed to the layout of track and to the overhead electrical equipment at Wood Street if this had continued to be the prospective Victoria Line terminus. This work would have been very costly and would have caused serious disturbance to Eastern Region services and passengers while it was being carried out.

The Walthamstow terminus of the Victoria Line would now be under the existing Eastern Region Hoe Street station, where interchange would be provided between the Victoria Line at low level and the Eastern Region services above. Through passengers between the Victoria Line and Highams Park and Chingford would not be placed at any great disadvantage by these revised arrangements though it meant that they would change at a different station and lose the cross-platform interchange originally planned. Against this, the revision of plans had the effect of making a reduction of some £1,400,000 in the capital cost of the new line.

The change of alignment needed Parliamentary powers before it could be put into effect, but the announcement had the effect of removing the uncertainty which had been holding up building developments in the Walthamstow area.

The London Transport annual review for 1961 (published in July 1962) stated again the view of the Executive that in the light of prospective traffic developments in London they must continue to press for the construction of the Victoria Line if they were to fulfil their statutory duty to provide adequate services in the London area. At last, on 20 August 1962, the Government gave its sanction to the construction of the line.

III The Victoria Line

ALTHOUGH the general route of the line has already been given, it is time now to examine the Victoria Line, as approved, in more detail, and see just what it was proposed to build from the north-east suburbs, across central London, to Victoria—and possibly beyond.

The line would be 10½ miles long and one of the biggest engineering jobs ever undertaken in London. It would involve complicated and extensive reconstruction, mostly underground, of the interchange stations which would be one of the line's most valuable features, making possible quicker journeys between many parts of London.

The whole of the line would be underground (except the rolling stock depot and its immediate approaches) and would run in twin tunnels each just over 12ft. in diameter and at an average depth of almost 69ft. There would be 12 stations as follows:

VICTORIA The new tube station serving this important gateway to the south would be built under the British Railways Southern Region station forecourt and the bus terminus, with escalator connections to the Southern Region and to London Transport's District and Circle Lines. The new ticket hall would link the existing District and Circle Line booking hall with stairs leading to the main-line station.

GREEN PARK Serving the Mayfair business area and giving interchange with the Piccadilly Line by subway and short stairs. There would be new escalators from the Victoria Line platforms to an enlarged ticket hall.

OXFORD CIRCUS Serving the centre of the West End shopping area. It is London's busiest peak-hour station. Much of the existing station would be rebuilt and a new ticket hall would be provided under the Circus itself with pavement entrances at each quadrant. There would be nine new escalators and cross-platform interchange between the Victoria and Bakerloo Lines in both directions at the existing Bakerloo Line level as well as subway interchanges with the Central Line.

WARREN STREET Serving a rapidly developing business area, it would have escalators to and from the Victoria Line platforms connecting with the existing escalators to and from the Northern Line and the street.

EUSTON Serving the rebuilt London Midland Region main-line station, it would give interchange with the Northern Line City and West End branches. The existing Underground station would be completely rebuilt, the lifts replaced by escalators, and cross-platform interchange would be provided between the Victoria Line and City trains of the Northern Line. The northbound tunnel of the City branch of the Northern Line was to be completely diverted without interfering with the City line service and work was at this time already well in hand on the reconstruction of the station, which had had to be undertaken partly because of the rebuilding of the main-line station above.

KING'S CROSS–ST. PANCRAS Escalators would be provided here to connect the Victoria Line with an enlarged sub-surface ticket hall giving access to the Metropolitan and Circle Lines. There would be subway interchange with the Northern and Piccadilly Lines, and new subway interchange with the Eastern and London Midland Region main-line stations.

HIGHBURY Cross-platform interchange was to be provided here with the Northern City Line (now known as the Highbury branch of the Northern Line)

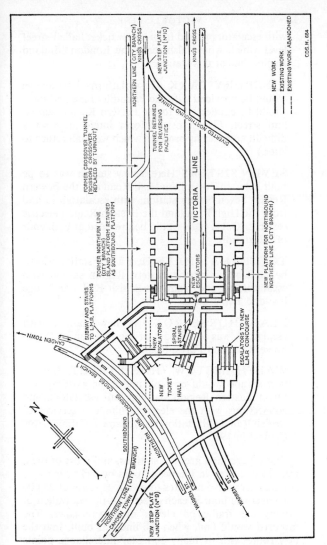

Reconstruction of Euston Underground Station: the new layout.

with escalators to and from a new ticket hall at street level which would also serve the London Midland Region line at this station.

FINSBURY PARK Cross-platform interchange would be provided with the Piccadilly Line and there would be connections to the Eastern Region station and street. (The cross-platform interchange set a difficult engineering problem which we shall return to later.)

SEVEN SISTERS Here a new station was to be built between Tottenham High Road and the Eastern Region Seven Sisters station, with escalators to and from the High Road and the Eastern Region electric services. Ticket halls would be provided at both ends of the station.

TOTTENHAM HALE Here a new station was to be built adjoining the Eastern Region station with escalators to and from the British Rail Cambridge line and Ferry Lane.

BLACKHORSE ROAD A new station, with escalators, was to be built at the junction of Blackhorse Road and Forest Road.

WALTHAMSTOW (HOE STREET) Here a new station would be built under the existing Hoe Street Eastern Region station, with escalators, and connections with the electric Chingford services of British Rail. (This station was renamed Walthamstow Central in 1968.)

These were (and are) the stations, and most of them were to be linked in the peak hours by eight-car trains running every two minutes to give a capacity of 25,000 passengers an hour in each direction—the equivalent of private car traffic on eleven motorway lanes. The motorist would find, when the line was built, that the new route with its many and easy interchange points with other lines would mean quicker travel than by car, especially for people in the north-east London areas of Chingford, Enfield, and Walthamstow and also—because of the better connections at Victoria—for people from Streatham and Brixton in the south. (This is even more true, today, with the Brixton extension of the Victoria Line built and open for traffic.)

The easy interchanges were always an important factor in justifying the line and much was, rightly, made of them at the time of the original announcement in 1962. Because of the original independence of the other, older, tube lines it has not always been possible to make interchange short and simple, and at some stations a long trek along subways and up-and-down stairs is inevitable. So far as physical circumstances allow, the Victoria Line was designed to cut out some of these long underground walks and considerable success has been achieved, sometimes with difficulty, as we shall see when we come to discuss the engineering work. 'Cross-platform' interchange was originally claimed at some stations but the term has now been altered to 'same-level'. This is because 'cross-platform' really applies only where passengers can alight from a train at one face of an island platform and board a train standing at the other face.

There *are* such interchanges on London Transport's surface and sub-surface lines—Mile End is a good example, where the Central Line comes up to sub-surface level to give interchange with the District Line —but on the deep tube lines there usually have to be individual platforms in individual station tunnels. At four stations—Oxford Circus, Euston, Highbury, and Finsbury Park—the Victoria Line station tunnels lie alongside some of the lines (Bakerloo, Northern (City branch), Northern (Highbury branch), and Piccadilly Lines respectively) with which they give interchange and the platforms are at the same level. The passenger virtually has to cross a wide platform to its other face, but as he has to go through one of a series of short tunnels in doing so it was thought less confusing to adopt the term 'same-level', which can also be used when platforms are a little farther apart but no stairs intervene. (As we shall see later, a similar same-level interchange station has also been provided at Stockwell on the Brixton extension.)

Some idea of the saving in time given by the Victoria Line by itself or with interchange to existing routes can be gathered from a few inner-London examples. The times quoted are for platform-to-platform journeys with an allowance for changing and waiting if a change is needed:

Victoria to Oxford Circus—a journey previously made only by changing Underground lines at Charing Cross— takes four minutes with two stations direct, instead of fourteen minutes previously with six stations plus a change.

Victoria to Green Park is a one-station journey taking two minutes, saving eight minutes or more on former bus journeys or a fifteen-minute walk across the Royal Parks.

King's Cross to Oxford Circus is possible with only three stations direct in five minutes, instead of four stations, plus a change, in ten minutes, or by bus.

Euston to Oxford Circus is two stations direct in four minutes, instead of four stations, plus a change, in nine minutes, or by bus.

Victoria to Baker Street is a four-station ten-minute journey with simple same-level interchange to the Bakerloo Line at Oxford Circus, instead of seventeen minutes with eight stations plus a change and escalator connection at Charing Cross.

The Victoria Line was also planned to open up new and direct travel routes into London from the north and south by connections with existing Underground and British Railways lines. Here again the new interchanges are speeding up, shortening and simplifying the daily journeys of thousands of Londoners.

At Euston the same-level interchange between the Victoria Line and the Northern Line (City branch) is unusual in that passengers board trains seemingly travelling in the opposite direction to continue their journey. Normally, in same-level interchange, trains depart in the same direction. By arranging for the tunnels of the two Victoria Line tracks to roll over at points south of Warren Street and north of King's Cross, the tracks are made to follow the right-hand rule of the road instead of the normal left-hand, through the intermediate stations. This allows, at Euston, the southbound Victoria Line, here pointing west, to have same-level interchange with the south-bound City section of the Northern Line—here pointing east—and the northbound tracks of both lines to run alongside each other in the same way. The ease of this interchange makes it worthwhile for passengers travelling from the Edgware and Barnet branches of the Northern Line bound for Oxford Circus or Victoria to use the City trains rather than the more heavily loaded Charing Cross trains. This further relieves the pressure on the Northern Line's West End service, especially at Tottenham Court Road, a busy transfer station for Oxford Street.

Chingford and Enfield passengers, with their electrified British Rail services into Liverpool Street, now get easy all-electric travel through to the West End by changing on to the Victoria Line at Walthamstow Central and Seven Sisters respectively.

Seven Sisters, which serves the busy Tottenham area, is only 15 minutes and six stations away from Oxford Circus, instead of 27 minutes and a change. Tottenham to Green Park takes only 19 minutes instead of 32, and Walthamstow to King's Cross is a journey of 17 minutes and six stations instead of 26 minutes, and Enfield to Oxford Circus takes 32 minutes instead of 44.

Passengers who do not use the Victoria Line have nevertheless felt its benefits, as peak-hour overcrowding on some of the busiest sections of existing Underground lines has been eased by the new line. For example, pressure on the Piccadilly Line has been re-duced by as much as one-third on the most congested stretch from Manor House to Holborn because pas-sengers who formerly joined the line at Manor House from the north-east suburbs are in the main using the new tube. Travel on the Central Line also is less crowded because of the transfer to the Victoria Line of significant numbers of passengers from the north-eastern suburbs who formerly joined the Central Line in the Woodford area, or at Leyton (having travelled by bus from Walthamstow), or at Liverpool Street (having travelled by Eastern Region suburban services).

The severe peak-hour overcrowding on the District Line between Charing Cross and Victoria, on the Nor-thern Line between Charing Cross and Tottenham Court Road, and on the Bakerloo Line between Charing Cross and Oxford Circus, is being eased by the new direct Victoria–Oxford Circus link given by the Victoria Line. The exception is the section of the Bakerloo Line between Baker Street and Oxford Circus, which, because of the easy interchange with the Victoria Line at Oxford Circus combined with the fast run to Victoria, attracts more rather than less traffic.

But all this was in the future when in 1962, as a fore-taste of what they could expect from their new Under-ground line, London Transport told passengers that the Victoria Line would be the most modern underground railway in the world, bringing a new age of travel to London. New ventilation equipment would keep the tunnels cool. Closed-circuit television would be installed at central stations to help in the control of passengers at peak hours and thus speed up the movement of everyone within the station. Automatic signalling by 'programme machines' (of which more later) was promised and there was a possibility of automatically-driven trains.

Such was the public face of the Victoria Line in August 1962. Now we will go behind the scenes.

iv Building the line: planning

THE ROUTE of the Victoria Line has not varied a great deal since its original inception, but several variations were examined before the final plans were made. One of these we have already mentioned—the proposal to transfer Manor House station from the Piccadilly Line to the Victoria Line and provide a new direct route for the Piccadilly Line between Finsbury Park and Turnpike Lane. This was dropped partly because it would have been expensive and difficult to programme—remembering that the Piccadilly Line would have had to be kept in commission the whole time and that large numbers of passengers use Manor House station—and partly because the influx of passengers at Manor House could well have resulted in the in-town section of the new line being overloaded. Another scheme was to route the line between Finsbury Park and King's Cross via the Nag's Head road junction, with a station at that busy point. This route would have been longer and more expensive, however, and the potentially important interchange at Highbury would have been lost—and this could be a very important interchange when the Great Northern suburban routes of the Eastern Region are electrified and the Region takes over the Highbury branch of the Northern Line. It will be a much easier interchange between the Eastern Region and Victoria Line trains than that at Finsbury Park, where the easy interchange is between the Piccadilly and Victoria Lines. A further route variation examined was between Green Park and Warren Street via Bond Street and Regent's Park. This will be recognized as a partial throwback to one of the earlier proposals, missing the traffic potentialities of Oxford Circus and serving less busily-used stations. This was abandoned partly for traffic reasons and partly because the interchange with the Central Line at Bond Street and with the Bakerloo

Line at Regent's Park would not have been as satisfactory as that at Oxford Circus.

There was also a proposal to take the line across the Lea Valley on the surface instead of in tunnel, which might have been financially attractive but was abandoned because of the difficulty in siting Seven Sisters station to advantage and the lack of nearby land suitable for a rolling stock depot. Seven Sisters is an important station both from the traffic point of view and because it is the logical place to turn some of the trains, just as some Piccadilly Line trains are turned at Wood Green or Arnos Grove, because the traffic is less at the outer end of the line and a full service throughout is not economically justified.

It goes without saying that careful estimates were prepared of the likely number of passengers beginning or ending their journeys or interchanging at each station. This arithmetic was hardly needed—it had all been done years before, as we have seen, and the new figures merely confirmed the old. Account had to be taken of passengers likely to be diverted from other London Transport or British Railways lines, or from buses, and of passengers likely to be attracted for the first time by the new service.

The technical planning already carried out by London Transport's New Works organization included finding out what sort of ground lay under the surface and what underground hazards, such as sewers, already existed. There is a deep layer of what is known as London Blue Clay underlying much of the London area and this is an almost ideal material in which to tunnel. It is relatively soft and yet will hold up without crumbling long enough after the tunnelling shield has passed to allow tunnel lining segments to be erected without needing any special support. The clay extends over all the area in which the Victoria Line has been built, though not at a uniform depth. The line had to be planned to keep within this clay layer as far as possible while avoiding other tube railways and sewers already in the layer and yet coming to suitable levels at interchange stations. At King's Cross there was only one possible level—a very tight squeeze between the Metropolitan and Circle Lines above and the Piccadilly Line below.

The geological survey and other sources were consulted and a cross-section in depth was prepared showing the upper and lower levels of the clay and the known existing obstructions. Starting from Victoria, the line breaks through the upper clay limit for some distance between Victoria and Green Park and dives below it shortly after leaving Warren Street, re-entering it just before reaching King's Cross. On this Victoria–King's Cross section the line keeps below a sewer just before reaching Green Park, where it passes just over the Piccadilly Line. It squeezes between sewers above and the Bakerloo and Central Lines below just before reaching Oxford Circus. The station tunnels themselves pass just over the Post Office railway. Just beyond Warren Street the Victoria Line passes below the Northern Line and at Euston it drops to the Northern Line level to give same-level interchange. At King's Cross there is a fantastic number of sewers (including the Fleet River) and suburban and Underground railway tunnels through which the Victoria Line had to thread its way—but more of this later.

From King's Cross to Highbury & Islington the line stays in the clay, and the only near obstacle is the Highbury branch of the Northern Line, approaching Highbury. The Victoria Line goes over the Highbury branch here, is at the same level in the station and then dives under the Highbury branch again on its way to Finsbury Park. Approaching Finsbury Park, the line keeps just below a group of sewers and then crosses the Piccadilly Line both south and north of the station. At both Highbury and Finsbury Park the two tunnels of the Victoria Line divide to give same-level interchange so that in some cases only one of the tunnels crosses under or over others. This will be explained in more detail later. At Finsbury Park, too, the Victoria Line emerges partially from the clay layer, but it enters it again almost immediately afterwards for a clear run to Seven Sisters and Tottenham Hale. At almost two-thirds of the distance from Tottenham Hale to Black-horse Road, the clay layer drops to the top of the tunnels, as it does again halfway between Blackhorse Road and Walthamstow Central.

The line rises 130ft. in the six miles from Victoria to Finsbury Park and then falls 100ft. to cross the Lea Valley. It then rises another 60ft. to Walthamstow Central.

Aerial surveys had been made of three of the routes proposed by the Working Party in their 1949 report, and as one of these was the Victoria Line it was pos-sible to correct existing ordnance maps from the survey to produce a strip map of the route showing a quarter-of-a-mile width. The main maps used were on the scale of 1in. to 88ft., but in some cases other, more up-to-date maps were enlarged to the same scale. The corrected strip map was then used as the basis of the plans of the route, and these were checked on the ground. This task and the preparation of the subsequent Parliamentary plans (showing a strip 300ft. wide) took 12 men a year.

In earlier tube railway construction care was taken to run the tunnels under streets as far as possible in order to minimize claims from property owners who might suggest the railway was affecting them. Time has shown this fear to be exaggerated and the Victoria Line has been planned to run on a much more direct route without particular regard to buildings above. This meant an increase in the number of properties which might have been affected either by the line passing under them or by compulsory purchase so that their sites could be used for engineering work such as sinking a shaft for materials, spoil removal, ventilation etc. The Parliamentary plans allow a certain margin for the railway to swing to one side of the route or the other if needed, and this is known as the 'limits of deviation'. Within these limits lay 3,300 properties which could have been affected in one way or another, but only 26 petitions against the plans were received. In all these cases terms were agreed before the Bill came up in the House of Commons.

To carry out works of this magnitude it is essential to have compulsory powers, for use if necessary, to acquire land for permanent occupation, e.g. for station buildings, for ventilation shafts, and for electrical sub-stations. It is also necessary to have temporary occupation, possibly for a period of some years, of land where working shafts can be sunk and materials stored. Provision for these things was included in the Bill before Parliament, so their positions had to be worked out in detail beforehand. Shafts were sunk in open spaces where possible to avoid unnecessary disturbance to buildings. There were such shafts in Finsbury Park and Green Park, for example, and in Cavendish Square, the headquarters for the extensive work at Oxford Circus, there was a shaft and a large stacking area. Where squares and parks were used, an undertaking was given to restore them as far as possible to their original condition, making due allowance for any permanent ventilation shafts, etc., which might be needed at the site.

After it had been decided where the stations would be and how the line could be built, the next thing was to consider how many extra tunnels would be needed for sidings and crossover points to enable the trains to work efficiently and how the stations should be laid out to give passengers the quickest and easiest route to and from their trains.

The site for the rolling stock depot had been decided already. It was to be at Northumberland Park, alongside the Eastern Region Lea Valley line to Bishop's Stortford and Cambridge. It was to be reached by an underground connection at Seven Sisters which would come to the surface just before reaching the depot. The trains would be maintained and stabled there, but it was necessary to have some trains at the other end of the line, at Victoria, to begin the service in the mornings—otherwise the trains from Northumberland Park would have to start out much earlier and run more or less empty to Victoria. The reverse would have to take place at night, the extra morning and evening running reducing by an hour or so the already short period in the small hours when no trains would run and all the maintenance work on track, signals, and tunnels would have to be carried out.

For this reason, it was decided that Victoria should have space to stable three trains in tunnels south of the station. It was also to have another siding tunnel of somewhat larger size with an inspection pit between the rails to enable trains to be examined and minor repairs made if required, giving four sidings in all. The outer tunnels were so sited that they could form running tunnels if an extension southwards were to be authorized at a later date—as it was—and the other two sidings were placed between them. Points and a scissors cross-over would enable any train to reach any siding.

Another scissors crossover was sited on the Green Park side of Victoria station to enable trains to cross from one running tunnel to another. There is another crossover at Warren Street. The tunnels required for these crossovers are among the largest and most impressive on the Underground.

There are no more sidings until King's Cross, where there is a single siding tunnel at the east end of the station, with connections to both running lines, to enable trains to be reversed or a defective train to be stabled until it can be moved to the depot. There is another crossover beyond Highbury & Islington station, and at Finsbury Park there is a connection with the Piccadilly Line. This is provided to enable Victoria Line trains to reach London Transport's main railway overhaul works at Acton and engineer's trains from Lillie Bridge to reach the Victoria Line.

At Seven Sisters there are three platform lines, the outer two being the main running lines and the centre track being used by reversing trains. This centre track continues to form one of the twin tracks to the depot, the second depot track, normally used by trains entering service, joins the main line running towards Victoria. There is a crossover connection between the two depot tracks at the depot end of Seven Sisters station and a connection at the same end between the centre track and the running line towards Walthamstow. The only other feature of this type is a crossover just before reaching Walthamstow Central.

Before we leave the tunnels, it should be said that the Victoria Line does not have tunnels of its present size just because the other tube railways have something very similar. Considerable thought was given to making the tunnels 17ft. in diameter, which would have made it possible to use rolling stock the same size as that on the District Line, which calculations showed to have a 10 per cent greater carrying capacity than tube stock at that time. To have done this, however, would have made it very expensive indeed to have provided interchange at Finsbury Park, Euston, and Oxford Circus. It could not have been done at all at King's Cross without expensive alterations to existing lines and a major diversion of the Fleet River. Most telling of all, the cost of tunnels has usually been held, as a rule-of-thumb calculation, to vary with the square of the diameter, so that the 17-ft. tube would have cost twice as much as the 12-ft. tube. The economics of the situation, therefore, were all against the 17ft.

Consideration was then given to a 14ft. 6in. diameter tube, which would have reduced some of the difficulties and the cost and still have allowed District-type stock to be used, though with reduced headroom. The point about this type of stock is that all the mechanism can be placed below the floor and there is full freedom to plan the layout of the seats. In tube stock there must be longitudinal seats where the wheels 'come up through the floor' and the space under every seat is packed with apparatus so that there is almost no latitude in planning the position and type of seats. The 14ft. 6in. tube was abandoned because it would have cost more to build than a 12-ft. tunnel (on the squaring principle) and because there would have been no means of getting the

C

stock to the Acton overhaul works. This would have meant providing some facilities for heavy overhaul at Northumberland Park, for a limited number of trains, which would have been difficult and could be uneconomic at this time.

The tunnel diameter chosen varies slightly with the type of lining, which we shall look at in detail later, but is generally 12ft. 6in., 12ft. 7in. or 12ft. 8in. (The smallest is 12ft. 2in.) This slight increase over the generally accepted 12ft. diameter of the London tube lines brings with it a considerable bonus—though this was not the reason for its choice, which depended on technical factors connected with driving and lining the tunnels. Experiments undertaken with conventional tube trains in tunnels of differing diameters showed that if the diameter could be raised to 12ft. 6in. the air drag acting on the trains would not be markedly different from that acting on a train in the open. This would mean savings in electric current and would also reduce the volume of air pushed ahead of the trains, which causes discomfort to passengers at some existing tube stations. Resistance to the passage of a train would be further reduced if the tunnel lining could be made smooth instead of ribbed as in conventional tunnels, and this, too, has been partially possible.

The design of the stations also presented problems, especially as so many of the Victoria Line platforms were to be built as additions to existing stations and there had to be convenient interchange with the older sections. An important preliminary was to decide the length of the new platforms, and, since the one depended on the other, the length of the Victoria Line trains.

Research teams were given the task of investigating the capacity of rolling stock; of stairways, passageways and escalators; and of a tube line in an endeavour to fix some of the basic data.

One of the most interesting of these investigations was that into stairways and passageways. To simulate traffic in subways the co-operation of a well-known public school for boys was sought and the boys were asked to feed into passageways of different widths—simulated by fencing which could be moved as required—while the speed of flow was calculated. Making allowances for the fact that schoolboys engaged knowingly in an artificial test are not strictly comparable with a cross-section of the public going about their everyday affairs, it was possible to produce curves showing the width of passageway needed for any desired flow per minute. Observations of normal passenger flow in station sub-ways showed that stairways were the main obstacle to even speed and needed to be half as wide again as the subway if this loss of speed was to be avoided. In foot-ways more than 4ft. wide passenger flow proved to be at a rate of 3·6 m.p.h., but upward stairs brought the speed down to 1·8 m.p.h. and downward stairs were not much better at 2·2 m.p.h.

One of the maxims for a high-capacity railway is to have the entrance towards one end of the platform and the exit towards the other, so as to rationalize the flow of passengers along the platform as much as possible and avoid conflicting streams. Similarly, where busy stations are fairly close together it is desirable that the points of entry and exit should be staggered so that they are opposite different cars of the train. This distributes the passengers along the train to some extent and assists in passenger flow on the platforms. The object of all this is to load and unload passengers as quickly as possible, for where stations are close together the deciding factor in the number of trains that can be operated in peak hours is the rate of passenger flow through the car doors. During a 30-second station stop, 900 passengers should be able to pass through the doors of an eight-car train.

Although these points were kept in mind when the Victoria Line stations were being designed there were in practice considerable limitations caused by, again, the need to join the new platforms to existing installations. These limitations also hampered the inclusion of 'saw-tooth' track profiles at stations. These give a rising gradient before the platform to help trains to slow down and a falling gradient beyond the station so that trains gather speed quickly.

Large-scale works were, of course, planned for existing stations to enable them to cope with the extra passengers and additional interchange traffic, and these will be dealt with later.

v The great experiment

NO NEW SECTION of tube railway had been built by London Transport since 1940, when hostilities had brought the massive works of the immediate pre-war years to a halt. The last new tube railway across central London had been opened more than half a century ago, in 1907. The only method of tunnel lining regarded as suitable for the later extensions, as well as the 1907 line, was bolted cast-iron segments grouted with cement to fill up the gap between the lining and the walls of the surrounding excavations. Concrete segments had been used on part of the Central Line extensions completed at the beginning of the war, but these were designed for use in the same way as the cast iron and were essentially a substitute measure made necessary by wartime demands for iron. Bolted cast-iron linings, grouted as described, are still one of the best types, especially in difficult ground. Other methods offered savings in both time and money if they could match up to the high standards of the conventional lining, but they entailed using new methods of tunnelling. London Transport's engineers, led by C. E. Dunton, the Chief Civil Engineer, considered it necessary that these new methods should be tested so that the quickest and most economical form of tube tunnelling available could be used where appropriate for the Victoria Line. A suitable area where there was little valuable property above, and the tunnels could be expected to be in good clay throughout, was chosen. Contracts were placed early in 1960 for a great experiment—the building of experimental lengths of twin tunnel, one running from Finsbury Park to Manor House and the other from Netherton Road (Tottenham) to Manor House, where the two lengths of tunnel would meet. The tunnels would follow the route of the Victoria Line and be capable of being used as part of it, if and when the construction of the line was approved. The total length of twin tunnel involved was about one mile, and the cost just over £1 million. Working sites were set up and shafts sunk at the corner of Netherton Road and Seven Sisters Road (Tottenham), and in Finsbury Park itself, near the Eastern Region main line from King's Cross to the north.

The 25-ft. diameter Netherton Road shaft, 60ft. deep, was to be a permanent part of the Victoria Line to be used eventually for ventilation and emergency stairs. From its foot an access tunnel was built a short distance to the line of the running tunnels, where chambers large enough to permit the assembly of the 'drum-digger' rotary shields were excavated by miners using pneumatic spades. The chambers were lined with the proven bolted cast-iron segments. When the shields began operations, excavated spoil was brought to the surface by a crane which lifted skips from 2-ft. gauge bogies which brought them, in trains hauled by battery locomotives, along the completed section of the tunnels. The skips were loaded by conveyor belt from the rotary cutters at the working face and were emptied on to the ground at the surface, the spoil then being loaded into lorries by a mobile shovel.

At the Finsbury Park working site the shaft was 15ft. in diameter and 60ft. deep. As at the other site, an access tunnel ran from its foot to the line of the running tunnels and there were two shield-assembly chambers. The running tunnels here were built on a falling gradient of 1 in 47 and loaded spoil skips were hauled to the end of the access tunnel by an electric winch in the shield-assembly chamber.

The skips tipped the spoil on to a belt conveyor in the access tunnel, to be carried to the foot of the shaft where it was hoisted to the surface by a continuous vertical bucket elevator, the buckets of which were warmed by hot air to prevent the clay sticking to the metal. Here again, a mobile shovel was used for loading the spoil into lorries.

The 'drum-digger' type of shield, already mentioned,

was developed by Kinnear Moodie & Co. Ltd. and Arthur Foster Constructional Engineers Ltd. It had already been used previously for tunnelling work for the Metropolitan Water Board's Thames to Lea Valley water tunnel—a scheme which also had involved building a considerable trial length of tunnel. The experimental railway tunnels were of much greater size than the water tunnel, and the drum-digger shields were therefore on a larger scale. The general design, however, remained unaltered. Two sizes were used, one for the tunnels on the Finsbury Park – Manor House section lined with concrete-block segments of a new pattern, and the other for the Netherton Road–Manor House section where a new type of flexible-jointed cast-iron lining without bolts and with much shallower flanges than those of bolted linings was tried. The drum-digger for the concrete-lined tunnels had an external diameter of 14ft. and that for the cast-iron-lined tunnels 13ft. 1in.

A drum-digger consists essentially of two drums, with the leading end of the outer drum bevelled to form a cutting edge. Within the main drum is a smaller rotating drum carried on roller races and provided with a thrust ring to take the axial load from the rotating cutters. The cutting teeth themselves are mounted on arms at the front of the shield, each carrying removable teeth. The arms are mounted at the outer edge of the inner rotating drum, so that they cut the area in front of the space between inner and outer drums; the area in front of the inner drum is cut by teeth mounted on a removable arm placed across it. The teeth can be replaced after hand-mining a small cavity in front of the arms. The inner drum, and the cutting teeth with it, can be turned at speeds of up to 4 r.p.m. by hydraulic motors.

The forward movement of the shield is given by hydraulic rams arranged at equal spacing round the periphery of the shield at the rear and pushing against the last completed tunnel ring. These rams, which operate at a working pressure of about 2,000 lb. per sq. in., are individually controlled by an operator standing within the shield casing behind the rotating inner drum.

The ram operator is provided with sighting guides which show him whether the shield is on the correct line and level and he can apply or reduce pressure to any of the rams to correct any tendency to deviate to the right or left or up or down. The sighting devices used on the two shields in the experimental tunnel were different, the more elaborate being arranged so that the ram operator could sight the image of a cross of light on a graduated mirror to obtain a direct indication of any deviation from true line or level. The source of light was a lamp, placed farther back along the tunnel, from which a beam passed through two cruciform slits in markers fixed to the roof of the tunnel and placed in precisely the correct position by the use of surveying instruments. When driving a curved length of tunnel, the mirror sighting device could be adjusted against a scale, after each ring of lining was erected, to keep the shield on its proper alignment. The accuracy of the drive is more difficult to maintain with mechanical excavator shields than with the Greathead type, and London Transport allows a tolerance of $\pm 1\frac{1}{2}$in.

The clay is cut by the rotating teeth of the shield and guided by scoops and paddles into a hopper from which it drops on to the end of an inclined electrically driven belt conveyor. This discharges on to the main horizontal belt conveyor which carries the excavated clay back along a staging. In the experimental tunnel it was discharged into skips on 2-ft. gauge track on each side of the horizontal conveyor.

Under the conveyor staging was a 200-h.p. electric motor driving pumps to provide hydraulic power for the shield motors. A separate $12\frac{1}{2}$-h.p. electric motor supplied hydraulic power for the rams. At the sides of the conveyor belt, at the shield end, were electric hoists for handling tunnel-lining segments.

To the rear of the conveyor and the hydraulic power unit the tracks on each side converged into one and passed down a short ramp to join the main tunnel track.

The whole of this apparatus, from immediately behind the shield to the rail ramp at the rear, was mounted on an articulated trailing platform, attached to the rear of the shield and drawn forward as the shield advanced. When the rams had pushed the shield forward the width of a ring of tunnel lining, i.e. 2ft., they were retracted. A tunnel-lining ring was then built in the space between the last completed ring and the rear of the shield. When this had been completed the whole cycle recommenced, the rams pushing against the newly installed ring.

Because of the considerable heat generated at the working face, the oil in the hydraulic system of the earlier shields of this type has to be cooled. This is done by providing a heat exchanger, cooling water being fed to the exchanger by piping from the nearest shaft. On the return circuit the water is taken to the head of the shaft and passed through a cooler before being returned to the tunnel. The pipes of the cooling water circuit, like the power leads to the working face, have to be extended from time to time as work progresses. (Improved design has eliminated the need for cooling in later models.)

The drum-digger proved capable, in good conditions, of advancing more than 60ft. a day, working three 8-hr. shifts, over long periods—a much higher speed than had ever been maintained before in building a tube railway tunnel. The maximum length driven with flexible-jointed cast-iron linings in an 8-hr. shift was 36ft. and 476ft. the maximum for one week. With the concrete linings it was 360ft. in a week.

Discussions with London Transport's two firms of consulting engineers, Sir William Halcrow & Partners and Messrs. Mott, Hay & Anderson, had resulted in a decision to line just over half the tunnels with a flexible-jointed cast-iron lining designed by the latter, and the remainder with a concrete lining designed by the former. Both types depended on their being expanded against the surrounding clay immediately each ring was completed and while the clay remained self-supporting. The

Eastern Region of British Railways had built new tunnels for the East Coast main line at Potters Bar using concrete linings of unreinforced concrete, giving some experience with this material, but some questions could only be answered, for both types, by actually building a tube tunnel using them. The cast-iron flexible-jointed lining was designed as a result of a series of experiments in producing a form of cast-iron lining which could be expanded against the tunnel sides and needed no grouting. The joints allow a certain amount of rotation between segments during expansion. Once a lining of this type was devised it had to be tested in practice, and, with the co-operation of the Central Electricity Generating Board, London Transport paid, in 1958, for the erection of 20 rings of the new lining in a shield-driven tunnel used for water circulation at the CEGB's Belvedere Generating Station. The tunnel, of 14ft. internal diameter, was the nearest thing possible to a tube railway tunnel. The experience was useful in that modification of the proposed handling and jacking methods arose from it.

Flexible-jointed cast-iron segments, unbolted, were used for lining the tunnels built from the Netherton Road site by Edmund Nuttall Sons & Co. (London) Ltd. There are six segments, each 1in. in thickness, to every 2-ft. tunnel ring. One end of each segment is concave and the other convex, so that the ends of the segments form knuckle joints, each fitting into another.

The segments were put into place in the space left behind the shield when the rams were withdrawn, the two forming the invert, i.e. the bottom of the tunnel, being laid first, then the side segments. Finally, the segments forming the roof were manhandled into place and held by 'needles' mounted at the rear of the shield. The two segments forming the floor of the tunnel were cast with small recesses at their upper ends and, when the segments had all been erected, hydraulic jacks were fitted into these recesses and a force of 15 tons per jack applied to the ring segments, expanding them against the clay outside. (The pressure was reduced to 12 tons in later stages of the work.) This expansion created a small gap between the segments forming the sides and those forming the invert of the tunnel, and into each of these gaps were placed first two cast-iron knuckle pieces shaped to conform to the contour of the segments below and then two pairs of cast-iron taper packings which held the whole ring firmly in place when the pressure of the jacks was released. The jacks were specially made for this work by Young's Lifting Appliances and had a hand pump common to the two jacks on opposite sides of the tunnel.

The segments have shallow interior ribs enlarged to form perforated lugs at regular spacing round the periphery of the ring for handling purposes and to provide for the fixing of signal equipment, cable brackets, tunnel lighting, etc. The internal diameter of this type of lining, from rib surface to rib surface, is 12ft. 8in. This is somewhat more than is absolutely necessary but the external diameter is the same as that required for the conventional cast-iron lining used on certain lengths where there are junctions, cross-passages, or other special features.

The conventional lining, of 12ft. internal diameter, has deep recesses which can be used to accommodate comparatively bulky signal equipment and other apparatus. The recesses in flexible-jointed cast-iron lining are shallow, so that all equipment necessarily stands out from the inner surface of the tunnel lining.

The pre-cast concrete lining of the other half of the tunnels, built by Kinnear Moodie & Co. Ltd., was also of a new type. The tunnel itself was driven by the larger of the two drum-diggers, giving space for a tube of 12ft. 6in. internal diameter with a lining of pre-cast concrete segments, of which various thicknesses—from 4½in. to 9in.—were tested. (The final thickness used for the Victoria Line is 6in.)

Each tunnel ring was made up of 14 identical segments having one cross joint face convex and the other concave, so that they fitted together with knuckle joints similar to those used for the iron segments. When the 14 segments were assembled a gap of about 7in. remained at the top. This gap was filled by a pair of reinforced concrete folding wedges having plane contact faces and concave and convex faces respectively in contact with the segments on each side. The wedge with the wide end nearer to the shield was driven home by a pair of small hydraulic rams while the other wedge was held in position. These two wedges held the whole ring firmly in place. The concrete segments were cast with four holes equally spaced round the interior circumference for use in handling in the tunnel and later, using expanding bolts, for fixing tunnel equipment, serving the same purpose as the ribs of the cast-iron segments. The concrete segments were handled by hoists at the working face, an expanding bolt placed in one of the holes being used to lift them. They were lifted into their correct positions by a manipulator arm mounted at the rear of the shield and held in place by pull-out 'needles' until the wedges were driven into position.

No grouting was used with either of the tunnel linings in the experimental section and there was nothing between the rings, except that wood packing pieces were inserted between the cast-iron segments to distribute the thrust of the shield rams.

With bolted cast-iron linings, the connections between segments turn the whole of the structure into a single entity as far as electrical continuity is concerned: the tube forming an electrical shield for its contents. This is important where a tube railway runs, say, parallel with a line of British Railways electrified at 25,000V, 50 cycles and induced currents are possible. The new cast-iron lining, with its separate rings, can be joined electrically by inserting self-tapping screws to connect each ring with its neighbour, but the problem with concrete segments is greater. Here, in such circumstances, a continuous 'cage' of braided copper strips has to be applied to the concrete walls.

In the event, it was decided that bonding with screws or screening with copper could be left until circumstances made it clear what was needed, especially as many of the British Railways routes near which the Victoria Line would run seemed unlikely to be electrified in the near future. In the long run, it proved not to be required.

The experimental tunnels showed that the best thickness for concrete segments was 6in. and that the 'knuckle' joints used between the segments needed modification to ensure that they made proper contact. One of the firms of consulting engineers decided to reinforce the joint and the other to modify the design, with good results in each case. The 'jacking pockets' procedure used to expand the cast-iron linings proved superior to the folding wedges used with the concrete, and the concrete segments were altered to allow these, too, to be expanded by jacks. The accuracy with which the shields could be driven allowed a further important modification in concrete segment design, those forming the bottom or 'invert' of the tunnels being reshaped to form a base for the track. This greatly reduced the amount of concrete which had to be placed afterwards.

The cast-iron segments needed no modification and were adopted for the Oxford Circus–Victoria section of the line, where their marginal advantages offset the extra cost as compared with concrete.

The £1 million experiment paid off handsomely. It resulted in changes in the estimates of the cost of tunnels in favourable ground which brought the cost of the Victoria Line down by £3 million, as well as leaving as a legacy a mile of completed twin tunnels on the route of the Victoria Line.

VI Work in hand

AT THIS STAGE, the Government had still not approved
the start of work on the Victoria Line itself, but London
Transport had to make certain decisions in anticipation
of eventual approval. One was that London Transport
would place orders for the tunnelling shields and tunnel-
lining segments so that these would be ready when
contracts for the tunnelling itself could be placed, and
delays while each contractor obtained his own shields
and segments would be obviated. Bulk orders for the
lining segments would also ensure a lower price.
Another decision was to go ahead with the necessary
contract drawings and preliminary programmes of
work, for the alterations at King's Cross, Oxford
Circus, and Euston would be very extensive and would
have to be phased to allow passengers full use of the
stations while they were carried out.

At Euston, the necessity of replacing the lifts, which
had reached the end of their useful life, meant that
reconstruction of the Underground station had to be
undertaken before the authorization of the Victoria
Line. The scheme incorporated, necessarily, provision
for the Victoria Line platforms, for the station had to
be treated as a whole. The Underground station at
Euston, served already by the Charing Cross and City
branches of the Northern Line, was used by nearly 11
million passengers a year, and all these must still be
accommodated during the reconstruction work. The
completed station was to have a new sub-surface ticket
hall, four flights of twin escalators, and new interchange
subways. One of the new escalators was to pass directly
below the site of the famous Doric Arch, due for
demolition under the main-line station reconstruction
scheme. The Arch is commemorated in tile patterns in
the walls of the new Underground platforms. A new
platform was needed, with a considerable tube tunnel

diversion, for the northbound City branch of the Northern Line so that the Victoria Line platforms could be built between those of the City branch to give easy interchange. The first contract for work at the station was placed in 1961 with John Cochrane & Sons Ltd. Two further contracts for civil engineering work at Euston were let in June 1963 to A. Waddington & Son Ltd. and Charles Brand & Son Ltd.

With the authorization of the Victoria Line on 20 August 1962, London Transport was as well-prepared as possible in all the circumstances. The longest and most complicated task of the whole programme was that at Oxford Circus, and tenders were issued at once for some of the work there, including the essential task of finding out exactly where the many services—gas and water mains, electricity supply and Post Office cables, etc.—lay beneath the surface of this busy intersection. The work meant digging trenches across the surface of the Circus in a 'search pattern', working mainly at night for six months after the main traffic flow on the roads was over and either filling in or roofing over the trenches before 06 30 each morning to let the day's traffic flow again. Only on Sundays could work be done in the daytime.

This exploration work was a preliminary to selecting the sites for 25 supports for a steel 'umbrella' bridge, planned to cover the whole of Oxford Circus and carry the road traffic while the tube station was reconstructed underneath. The contract was let to Mitchell Bros. Sons & Co. of Victoria Street, SW1, and the work of drilling in the road began on the night of Thursday, 20 September, only one month after the authorization of the project.

Meanwhile London Transport had called a Press Conference for the day after the Government authorization was announced and full details of the Victoria Line appeared in the national, local and technical Press. The small exhibition site in the ticket hall at Charing Cross was converted to a cinema and a colour film of the experimental tunnels, 'Experiment under London', was shown eight times a day, free, for all Londoners interested in their future new line—and very many of them were. From 10 October a special exhibition was mounted on the same site featuring as its main attraction a large-scale cutaway model of Oxford Circus station as it would be when completed. So detailed was this model that even the posters on the platform walls were to the correct scale. It is now in the Science Museum, South Kensington.

One of the proposals for the Victoria Line concerned the use of closed-circuit television for crowd control, an idea already tried on a small scale on, for example, the Stockholm Underground. London Transport now went ahead with a full-scale experimental installation of television equipment at Holborn, one of the Underground's busiest stations, served by both the Piccadilly and Central Lines and handling some 32 million passengers a year. Cameras were set up on all four platforms, in the ticket hall, and at the foot of the lower flight of escalators leading to the Piccadilly Line. An operator, sitting at a control console in a special 'crow's nest' compartment built on the wall of the concourse at the foot of the main escalators, can switch the pictures from any of the cameras on to three monitor screens in front of him. Three of the cameras have remote control of pan and tilt, so that the operator can turn them to pick up anything which attracts his attention or to accord with morning or evening passenger flow. The 'crow's nest' has one-way glass, so that the operator also has a direct view of the main escalators— the only four-escalator bank at any London Transport station.

If the pictures show that pressure is building up at any point the operator can warn the station staff by telephone or he can switch on a microphone and address passengers direct through the station public address equipment.

Another innovation tried out at Holborn in readiness for the Victoria Line was a passenger information service which allows a passenger, from a 'head booth' similar to those now extensively used for telephones, to ask the television operator for information about the train service, etc. The operator answers by means of a 'talk-back' loudspeaker in the booth. (This service was later extended to the next station, Russell Square, in the heart of a tourist hotel area.)

Now, with the Victoria Line work just beginning to get into swing, on 10 January 1963 the Underground celebrated its 100th birthday. It was appropriate that London's Underground, pioneer of the many through-out the world, should be starting to grow an important new member and that one of the prime tasks of that member should be to connect, and enable better use to be made of, the lines which had gone before.

The next stage was the placing of a series of important contracts, tenders for which had been prepared and issued in the few months since authorization. First of these was a £5 million contract for cast-iron tunnel-lining segments placed with Stanton & Staveley Ltd. of Nottingham. Under the terms of the contract, Stanton & Staveley sublet one-third of the order, worth about £1·6 million, to Head Wrightson Iron Foundries Ltd. of Stockton-on-Tees, Co. Durham. This was the biggest single contract to be placed in connection with the Victoria Line. The cast-iron segments were for use in sections of the running tunnels, junctions, stations (totalling two miles in length) and escalators, concourses, subways, and ventilation shafts. A further contract for special type cast-iron segments worth £104,000 was placed with Harland & Wolff of Glasgow. More than 100 different diameters and types of rings were to be needed for the Victoria Line, some as much as 35ft. in diameter for crossover tunnels and junctions, and then down in size through escalator shafts, station and running tunnels to pedestrian subways, ventilation ducts, and still smaller openings.

Shortly after came contracts worth more than £500,000 for sixteen tunnelling shields, nine for the running and seven for the station tunnels. Eight of the shields were to have hydraulically operated rotary

D

cutters and Sir Robert McAlpine and Sons Ltd. were to build four of these shields to their own pattern, already proved successful on the Toronto Underground works. Kinnear Moodie & Co. Ltd. were to supply the other four. These were their 'drum-digger' type of shield and included the two used for the experimental tunnels built under Finsbury Park, reconditioned for their new tasks.

The contract for the ninth running tunnel shield, for use with hand power tools, went to Joseph Westwood & Co. Ltd. This shield was for use at Highbury where work on the diversion of a section of the northbound tunnel on the Highbury branch of the Northern Line, to give better interchange with the Victoria Line, was due to start shortly. Because of the larger section of the Highbury branch tunnels, this shield was designed to produce a tunnel of 16ft. internal diameter.

All seven of the station tunnel shields were to be built by W. Lawrence & Son (London) Ltd. and were of the Greathead type. They were much larger than the other shields because station tunnels are more than 21ft. in internal diameter. With these shields the clay is excavated with power-driven hand tools, but they are moved forward by hydraulic rams pressing against the completed rings of tunnel linings behind.*

A contract worth about £700,000 for concrete lining segments was placed with Kinnear Moodie and Co. Ltd., completing orders for tunnel linings required for the new line. Concrete segments were to be used for about 60 per cent of the running tunnels and the cast-iron segments, already ordered, would line the remaining running tunnels, as well as junctions, stations, escalators, concourses, and subways.

The first big engineering contracts were issued in March 1963. One, worth £682,000, was placed with F. J. C. Lilley (Contractors) Limited of Glasgow for building a half-mile section of running tunnel at Highbury with the 16-ft. shield already mentioned and for

*Altogether, 32 shields were used—eight mechanical excavator shields and nine Greathead type for running tunnels, and 15 shields for station work.

building a 460-ft. station tunnel with its associated passageways and concourse. The contract included the difficult work of building tunnel junctions round an existing tunnel while trains continued to run as usual. This entailed building a protective steel hood, mounted on rails, above the existing track. The extra diameter could then be excavated and the old tunnel lining removed while trains ran safely under the hood, which was moved along its rails as the work progressed.

A second contract, announced at the same time, was for the first stage of the work at the terminus of the new line, Victoria, involving the construction of stairs, subways and a shaft for a bank of two escalators to link the existing District Line platforms with those of the Victoria Line. The District Line platforms were also to be lengthened by 68ft. at the eastern end. Work on this first stage, which began on 22 April, was programmed to continue by day and night. It necessitated a small alteration to Wilton Road at the approach to Victoria Street, where the carriageway was widened, taking advantage of the wide pavement. Gas and water mains, and electricity and post office cables which lay beneath the road had to be diverted, and a shop at the junction of Victoria Street and Wilton Road had to be demolished so that part of the District Line tunnel arch could be removed and a new roof constructed over the lengthened station. (The shop was later reinstated.) This contract, worth £467,000, was let to Marples, Ridgway and Partners Ltd. of London.

The second stage of the Victoria scheme, undertaken by the same firm as an extension of the original contract, began later and involved the construction of the new Victoria Line station itself as well as the building of a large new sub-surface ticket hall beneath the Southern Region station forecourt and the bus terminus. This ticket hall is connected with the main-line station by stairways, with the Victoria Line platforms 59ft. below ground by a bank of three escalators, and with the District and Circle Lines ticket hall by a new and wider subway on the line of the earlier one which provided interchange with the Southern Region terminus. The new hall may eventually be connected to the Greater London Council pedestrian subways in the area.

Every Underground line must have at least one depot for its rolling stock, and that for the Victoria Line, as we have already seen, was to be at Northumberland Park alongside the Eastern Region line up the Lea Valley from London to Cambridge. The depot—the first to have covered accommodation for all trains—had already been designed and the contract for its first stage, worth £775,000, was placed in July 1963 with J. L. Kier & Co. Ltd. of London. This included heavy earthworks, the installation of drainage, the foundations for the depot buildings, and the reinforced concrete covered way and portals to the tube tunnels where they rise to the surface. From the junction at Seven Sisters to the depot entrance the connecting line is about $1\frac{1}{4}$ miles long, with about half a mile in tunnel.

The main building is 470ft. long and has 12 tracks each able to take a full-length tube train. Nine of the tracks have pits and the other three, over which the roof is higher, are 'lifting' tracks with overhead gantry cranes for lifting the car bodies from the bogies for inspection or maintenance. The stabling accommodation, at the north end of the depot, consists of a building 900ft. in length containing 11 sidings each of which can take two eight-car trains. There is workshop, office, and staff accommodation, mainly in a two-storey block attached to the main building.

Movement of trains into and out of the depot is regulated from a control tower near the south end of the depot where the fans of tracks converge into four, two of which run straight to the incline leading to the tunnels. The other two tracks pass through washing plants before joining the incline tracks. All trains are washed externally by going through the washing plants as they come out of service, but they normally go into service via the direct tracks, by-passing the washing machines.

VII Bridging Oxford Circus

AT 13 30 on Saturday, 3 August 1963, Oxford Circus and most of the surrounding streets were closed to all road traffic and to all non-residents. At 06 30 on Tuesday, 6 August, the streets were opened again. In those 65 hours of the Bank Holiday weekend London Transport's engineers and contractors had built an 'umbrella' bridge weighing 600 tons and covering an area of 2,500 sq. yds. to carry traffic four ways over Oxford Circus while a new upper concourse for London Transport's Underground station was built underneath.

The plan was to have a large circular sub-surface ticket hall beneath Oxford Circus itself, with a pavement stairwell entrance at each of the four quadrants. To avoid disrupting road traffic over a long period it was decided, as mentioned in a previous chapter, to build a steel 'umbrella' over the whole of the Circus to carry the traffic while the ticket hall was being built. The digging of exploratory pits and headings to discover the exact whereabouts of the many pipes and cables carrying the various services, water, gas, GPO telephones and TV cables, electric power, etc., beneath the crossroads had, as we know, begun only a month after the authorization of the Victoria Line, and this had enabled positions to be planned for 25 concrete cylinder foundations to carry the 'umbrella'. The pile foundations were sunk between 43ft. and 73ft. beneath the road surface during limited occupations of the roadway at nights and weekends.

The steelwork of the bridge itself was fabricated by Rubery Owen Ltd. in Staffordshire. It included 27 main girders up to 35ft. in length and 24 tapering girders to take the bridge from its full height down to ramp end panels to bring the bridge back to normal road level. There were also 197 steel panels of battle-deck construction, mostly 25ft. by 6ft. and weighing up to 5 tons each,

already laid with asphalt and chippings to form the
roadway itself. In all, there were 245 pieces of pre-
fabricated steelwork to be fitted into place. These were
brought to London and stacked at the south end of
Cavendish Square, near Oxford Circus. The pieces were
coloured either yellow for the North or blue for the
South and were numbered and stacked for systematic
erection by 'blue' and 'yellow' gangs of erectors.

In readiness for the weekend's work, fittings were
added to the cylinder foundations and other foundations
were prepared. Hoardings were erected in Regent Street
(North), and barriers, signs, and lamps for closing the
roads were prepared. Catering and sanitary arrangements were made for the 200 men who would be at
work in shifts during the weekend, and identity docu-
ments and badges were prepared to identify engineers
and workmen so that the police would allow them into
the closed area. The Metropolitan Police prepared and
publicized traffic diversion plans and London Transport
arranged and publicized bus and coach route diversions.
The St. Marylebone Borough Council, in conjunction
with the Westminster City Council, arranged the removal of traffic islands and bollards, and erected new
lamp standards.

On the night of Friday, 2/3 August, part of the hoarding in Cavendish Square was taken down in readiness
for the removal of the steelwork and traffic diversion
signs were erected but left covered. On the Saturday
morning the St. Marylebone Borough Council removed
all the traffic lights from the Circus and the Metropolitan Police took over the direction of traffic. At
13 15 the police, stationed at all the road approaches,
turned traffic on to the diversion routes. Traffic and
pedestrian barriers, signboards and notices, were put up
and all were in position at or just after 13 30. London
Transport had meanwhile closed the entrance to Oxford
Circus station west of Argyll Street and the Circus was
deserted except for the workmen.

The granite kerbs were removed from the Circus and
stacked in Regent Street (North) and the prepared

foundations were cleaned out. Steel stools were erected on top of the cylinder foundations. Two 30-man steel erector gangs, the North and South ('blue' and 'yellow') gangs, began to erect the steelwork brought forward as required by low-loader lorries from Cavendish Square. Beams, trusses, panels, ramp units, each numbered and coloured in accordance with the pre-arranged plan, followed one another to the site and were lifted by road mobile cranes and lowered into place.

The bridge itself was due for completion by noon on Monday, 5 August, and was actually completed by 12 15. Meanwhile, timber kerbs and splash barriers were being fixed and smooth joins were being made between the existing road surfaces and the ramps.

By Monday afternoon traffic lights were being fixed on the umbrella deck, traffic stop lines were being marked, and the granite kerbs previously removed were being replaced, this time on the umbrella deck. Meanwhile, general cleaning-up was in progress, permanent signs were being fixed, the asphalt ramp ends were being formed, and pedestrian crossings marked at the ends of the ramps.

In the final stage, from midnight on Monday until 06 30 on Tuesday, the timber pavement-decking at the south end of the hoarding in Regent Street (North) was completed and at 06 00 the traffic and pedestrian barriers began to be removed.

At 06 30 all the diversion signs were removed and the Metropolitan Police allowed the early morning traffic to move into Oxford Circus and over the bridge. First across was a small blue van, followed by a bus with the appropriate destination—'Victoria', on the blind. The umbrella, to be a feature of the London scene for nearly five years, was taking its first traffic 3ft. 6in. above the former road surface, and another step towards the Victoria Line had been successfully taken.

The bridge gave a full-width road from Regent Street (South) and from Oxford Street (East and West). The ramp to Regent Street (North) was to the west side only, the east side being closed and used as a working

site for building the new ticket hall and driving the
escalator shaft to the intermediate landing level—
through which shaft interchange passages and other
escalator shafts were constructed.

The bridge was designed under the direction of
C. E. Dunton, London Transport's Chief Civil Engineer, with Sir William Halcrow & Partners as consulting engineers. The main contractors were Mitchell
Bros. Sons & Co., who had also carried out the preliminary exploratory work. The cylinder supports were
provided by McKinney Foundation Ltd. as sub-
contractors. The fabrication of the steelwork for the
bridge was subcontracted to the Staffordshire firm of
Rubery Owen & Co. Ltd., and the erection itself to
Carter-Horseley Ltd. The asphalt work was carried out
by the Limmer & Trinidad Lake Asphalt Co. Ltd. and
traffic lights, kerbs, etc. were removed and replaced by
the St. Marylebone Borough Council, who also dealt
with traffic signs of a permanent nature. This was a
fine example of team work by all concerned, and the
bridge, when erected, was the most important single
Victoria Line symbol in the eyes of most of the public.
It rapidly became a London landmark pointed out by
Londoners to their friends from abroad as the sign of
Victoria Line progress.

The bridging of the Circus was immediately followed
by the letting of a further contract, worth nearly £3
million, for the civil engineering work at the station—
expected eventually to handle 40 million passengers a
year. The contractors were Kinnear Moodie & Co. Ltd.
and their task was to build the circular sub-surface ticket
hall beneath the Circus with the stairwell entrance at
each of the four quadrants; five new escalator shafts;
separate station tunnels and platforms for the Victoria
Line; passages, subways and concourses to give same-
level interchange between the new tube and the Bakerloo Line in both directions, and to improve interchange
at low level with the Central Line. They were to make a
three-pronged attack on the construction work—from
under the 'umbrella' itself, from the working site in

Regent Street north of the Circus, and from deep shafts already sunk in Cavendish Square.

One of the first tasks was the extensive diversion of the maze of gas and water mains, sewers, and electricity and Post Office cables which had been mapped as they criss-crossed the area under the Circus. The water mains and GPO cables were to be put into special tunnels to be driven under the new ticket hall from smaller working sites in the area and the others were to be carried round it. The sewers to be diverted to make room for the new station included the Marylebone Sewer, for which a new section more than 100yds. long had to be constructed.

The lack of open space round Oxford Circus made it necessary for Cavendish Square to be used as a main working site. The principal access shafts were located there and connected by temporary tunnels, driven for access purposes only, to the working areas alongside the Bakerloo Line platforms and elsewhere. The Regent Street site was kept as uncluttered by temporary works as possible.

This difficulty of access presented considerable problems. For example, columns 23ft. in length and girders up to 35ft. long and weighing as much as nine tons had to be lowered down at night through small gaps made by removing sections of the 'umbrella'. They were needed to support the new roof of the ticket hall and carry the future roadway. In these cramped circumstances, 19 columns, 66 main girders and something like 600 smaller girders were passed through the small openings into the space below. All the ready-mixed concrete for the roof of the ticket hall was delivered through similar gaps.

The other main problem at Oxford Circus was Peter Robinson's department store, which has three basements and massive column foundations, just under which one of the new Victoria Line station tunnels had to run. There was very little space between the footings of the foundations and the roof of the tunnel but a means had to be found of distributing the load over a

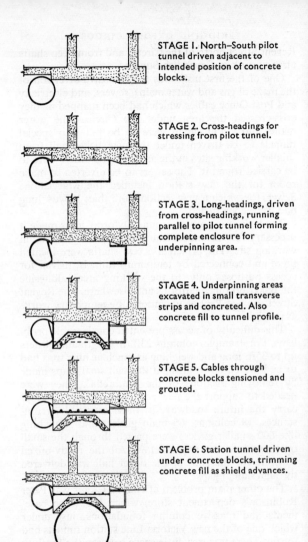

STAGE 1. North–South pilot tunnel driven adjacent to intended position of concrete blocks.

STAGE 2. Cross-headings for stressing from pilot tunnel.

STAGE 3. Long-headings, driven from cross-headings, running parallel to pilot tunnel forming complete enclosure for underpinning area.

STAGE 4. Underpinning areas excavated in small transverse strips and concreted. Also concrete fill to tunnel profile.

STAGE 5. Cables through concrete blocks tensioned and grouted.

STAGE 6. Station tunnel driven under concrete blocks, trimming concrete fill as shield advances.

Underpinning sequence—Peter Robinson's Store.
Courtesy: Mitchell Construction Kinnear Moodie Group Ltd.

wider area before tunnelling began. A 250-yd. tunnel was driven underneath the Bakerloo Line to give access to a point beneath the foundations from which a vertical shaft was constructed to reach them. From this point a pilot tunnel was driven parallel to, and just below, the foundation footings. Small rectangular headings were then driven to enclose the area, which was to be occupied by a post-stressed concrete raft to take and spread the load. Narrow headings were then driven beneath the foundations and at once filled with concrete in which were embedded steel ducts for the post-stressing cables. When the whole area had been concreted, high-tensile steel cables, colour coded to make sure that they emerged in the correct position without twists, were threaded through the ducts and anchored at one end. They were then stressed to a strain of 25 tons by a hydraulic tensioning machine powered by an electric pump and anchored at the free end when the tension came up to the correct figure. Once all the cables had been stressed, the tubes were filled with cement mortar.

The lowest section of the raft—or 'saddle', since it was shaped to lie over the tunnel—had been built of weak concrete, and when the shield driving the south-bound station tunnel, with a pressure of 800 tons in its rams, encountered the 'saddle' in November 1965, it scraped along beneath, taking off only an inch or so of the weak concrete layer to fit exactly into the saddle and take up the foundation load of the building. As the shield moved on, rings of special steel segments were placed behind it and expanded immediately against the tunnel sides to take up the load permanently.

The surveying and setting out of civil engineering works for an underground railway is of vital importance to the work as a whole, as well as difficult and tedious for those concerned. Special mention must be made here of the particularly onerous nature of this work at Oxford Circus, where all low-level works, including the underpinning of Peter Robinson's store, had to be set out by transferring lines from Cavendish Square.

In the August Bank Holiday weekend of 1966, the 'umbrella' bridge was lengthened by about 100ft. eastwards along Oxford Street to give space for further work near the surface, and the Circus was partly closed once again from 14 00 on Saturday, 27 August until 06 30 on Tuesday, 30 August. Southbound traffic along Regent Street could still cross the umbrella during this period. Pedestrians could use only the south-west sector of the Circus between Regent Street (South) and Oxford Street (West).

The work itself was fairly simple compared with the original erection, but entailed laying 31 new panels, up to 25ft. by 6ft. in size, on prepared foundations after removing the original Oxford Street ramp. After the erection of the new 100ft. length of 'umbrella', the ramp was installed again at the end of the new section.

It was not until the Easter weekend of 1968 that the bridge disappeared from the London scene. Once again the operation was carefully planned and explained to everyone concerned, including, by letter and public meeting, everyone who occupied premises in the area. Then the Circus was closed, for the third time, from about 23 30 on Thursday, 11 April, and the cranes, low-loading lorries, and gangs of workmen began to dismantle the bridge—with its extension, weighing some 1,200 tons. The bridge was taken to pieces by the same firm which had erected it, and work went so well that traffic was admitted to the newly revealed roadways several hours before the target time of 06 30 on Tuesday, 16 April. There was still plenty of work to be done below, and the quadrant entrances had still to be built, but the bridge over Oxford Circus had served its purpose and gone for sale to the highest bidder.

VIII More engineering

TO RETURN to the main stream of the Victoria Line story, in the autumn of 1963 civil engineering contracts were still being let. On 16 August a contract for Charles Brand & Son Ltd., worth £1·5 million, was announced. This covered the two-year task of driving twin running tunnels over a distance of 1⅔ miles at the northern end of the new line between Ferry Lane, Tottenham, and the sidings beyond the Walthamstow (Hoe Street) terminus, and also station tunnels at Hoe Street, Blackhorse Road, and Tottenham Hale. Over this section of the line the tunnels would run entirely through blue clay and the running tunnels would be lined with concrete segments. Cast-iron segments would be used for the station tunnels and the crossover at Walthamstow. The working site was in the car park of a sports ground at Ferry Lane, Tottenham, where, from the foot of a 50-ft. shaft, a short length of horizontal tunnel was to be dug to a chamber excavated on the line of the running tunnel in which the running tunnel shield would be assembled. Once the drive was in progress, spoil would be taken out by other shafts sunk in Pretoria Avenue, Walthamstow, and in the goods yard of the Eastern Region's Walthamstow (Hoe Street) station.

It was a year since the Government had given the 'go-ahead' for the Victoria Line, and London Transport took stock.

'During the past 12 months', the Press was told, 'London Transport's engineers have been working at top speed, acquiring and setting up working sites, preparing the detailed drawings, specifications and bills of quantities, sending out invitations to tender as fast as the civil engineering industry could take them, and letting contracts so that construction work could begin at a number of important points along the route of the 11-mile line.

'In this period contracts for special materials, plant and civil engineering works to the value of £17·5 million —or nearly one-third of the estimated cost of the line and its equipment—have been placed. They include orders for cast-iron and concrete segments for the tunnel linings and for mechanical and hand shields for driving the tunnels, and contracts for the building of about five miles of twin running tunnels, for extensive station works at Oxford Circus and Euston, for the diversion of existing tube lines at Highbury and Euston so as to give cross-platform interchange with the new tube, for works at Victoria, for preliminary works at King's Cross and for a train depot at Northumberland Park, Tottenham.'

Less than a week later came the announcement of another large contract to Charles Brand & Son Ltd. This was for the 1⅔ miles of twin running tunnels from Netherton Road (at the northern end of the experimental section of tunnels) to join up with the tunnels being built by the same firm from Ferry Lane, Tottenham, to Walthamstow. This new contract was worth some £2 million and included not only the running tunnels but also three 21-ft. diameter station tunnels for Seven Sisters station, complete with their cross-passages and platforms, a crossover tunnel, six tunnel junctions, and ventilation and cable shafts. This contract also included the twin tunnels of the branch from Seven Sisters to the train depot at Northumberland Park. Working sites were to be established at Page Green Common, Tottenham, where there were to be three 47-ft. shafts, and at Ferry Lane, Tynemouth Road and Westfield Road— the last two sites being for the construction of ventilation and cable shafts and tunnels.

The complexity of the Victoria Line work meant that a special organization had to be set up to programme the work and follow its progress to make sure that target dates were being met. London Transport decided early on to use modern network analysis methods and in September 1963 the appointment of Production-Engineering Ltd., as advisers on these methods, was announced. At that time, some 70 staff of London

Transport, the consulting engineers, and the tunnelling contractors had attended courses run by Production-Engineering Ltd., and 40 others were already taking courses.

In the event, networks showing main activities and sequences were produced for all civil engineering contracts and equipment processes. These were broken down into 54 sub-networks, each dealing with not more than 750 activities. At times, the number of activities being processed rose to 12,500. The earliest and latest starting and finishing dates for each activity were calculated by an IBM 7090 computer. This was the first time that critical path work analysis techniques had been applied on this scale on this side of the Atlantic.

The progress of the work as against the programme was watched by a working party which included representatives of all departments concerned and adjustments were made as required. Every eight weeks a progress and programming committee of chief officers and senior partners of the two firms of consulting engineers met, under the chairmanship of the Chief Civil Engineer, who acted as overall coordinator, to consider the reports of the working party.

In the closing months of 1963, more vital civil engineering contracts were let. John Mowlem & Co. Ltd. were to build the twin tunnels from Victoria to Oxford Circus, passing 65ft. down under the end of the Mall opposite the Queen Victoria Memorial outside Buckingham Palace, and continuing via Green Park into the heart of Mayfair. This contract, worth £2 million, also included the Victoria and Green Park station tunnels with their connecting passageways; two of the big, 'underground cathedral' crossover tunnels, one at each end of Victoria station; and four sidings at Gillingham Street beyond the Victoria terminus. One of the best-known of all the working sites was on this section—in a special enclosure in Green Park itself on the south side of the station. Also on this section was a shaft which already existed—the disused lift shaft of the former Dover Street station.

By the end of November, 70 per cent of the running tunnel contracts were let, including the £1·75 million task of building 1¾ miles of running tunnels between Oxford Circus and King's Cross. This was to be undertaken by Mitchell Bros. Sons & Co. Ltd. and included the station tunnels, a crossover tunnel, passageways, etc. at Warren Street and two station tunnels at Euston. A particularly interesting feature of this contract was that it included the 'roll over' between Oxford Circus and Warren Street where the northbound and southbound tunnels 'change sides' so that the desired interchange can be given at Euston with the City branch of the Northern Line. (The tunnels 'roll over' again to restore left-hand running on the King's Cross–Highbury section.)

It was known that the tunnels would pass through difficult ground between Oxford Circus and King's Cross, some of it gravel and some water-bearing, and because of this they were to be shield-driven with hand-held power tools instead of by mechanical digger shields, and lined with bolted cast-iron segments. In some sections, where there is water-bearing ground, the miners would have to work in compressed air to hold the water back from the new tunnels. Construction was to be carried out from three main working shafts—in Great Titchfield Street, Fitzroy Square, and Whitfield Place.

Now came the contract, with Kinnear Moodie & Co. Ltd., for the 2½ miles of tunnels between King's Cross and Finsbury Park (including the 'roll over' already mentioned). This work, worth £1·8 million, was expected to take 2½ years.

On 23 April 1964 it was possible for the first time to arrange for the Press to go down into the tunnels in force and show them miners at work under Oxford Circus. This was the first time a full-scale Press visit had been arranged, though a handful of journalists had descended in a swaying bucket into the experimental tunnels between Finsbury Park and Netherton Road two or three years before and had become the first

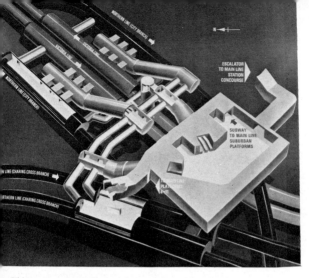

The new stations: Euston below the ground.

The new stations: The complexity of Underground Oxf

Steering a drum-digger shield by varying the pressure of hydraulic rams.

Erecting cast iron segments to line the tunnel behind a mechanical excavator shield.

A Kinnear Moodie drum-digger shield being hauled through a station tunnel at Green Park after completing a running tunnel drive from Victoria.

A McAlpine mechanical excavator shield breaks through into a station tunnel on completing a running tunnel drive.

A large-diameter Greathead-type tunnelling shield. When using shields like these, miners excavate the clay with powered hand tools.

Oxford Circus 'Umbrella' under construction.

Oxford Circus 'Umbrella' in full use.

Step-plate junction at Finsbury Park. (Above) One of the last trains over the old tracks. (Below) The new diversion in use. The mouth of the tunnel for the old track can be seen on the left.

A large-diameter crossover tunnel near Victoria.

A section of Victoria Line tunnel lined with conventional
bolted cast iron segments.

The new methods. (Above) A section of tunnel with articulated lining of unbolted cast iron segments. (Below) A section of tunnel lined with concrete segments.

A typical Victoria Line station platform—Seven Sisters.

In the new ticket hall at Oxford Circus.

Station Motifs

Walthamstow Central
by Julia Black

Seven Sisters
by Hans Unger

Finsbury Park
by Tom Eckersley

King's Cross
by Tom Eckersley

Euston
by Tom Eckersley

Warren Street
by Crosby/Fletcher/Forbes

Automatic fare collection. Inward and outward four-door gates at Seven Sisters. Note the excess ticket window.

Tripod or 'turnstile' type gates at Warren Street.

Her Majesty the Queen opening the Warren Street–Victoria section of the Victoria Line at Green Park station on 7 March 1969. Beside her on the platform is Sir Maurice Holmes, then Chairman of London Transport.

The Queen rides in a Victoria Line train on 7 March 1969 after opening the line. With her from left to right, are Sir Maurice Holmes, Mr. F. E. Wilkins (Chief Public Relations Officer, London Transport), Mr. Anthony Bull (Vice-Chairman, London Transport), and Mr. Richard Marsh (then Minister of Transport).

An automatically-driven Victoria Line train.

Interior of a Victoria Line driving car.

Interior of a Victoria Line trailer car. Note the all-longitudinal seating.

Mr. F. G. Maxwell, Operating Manager of London Transport's railways, shakes hands with Mr. William Harvey, train operator of the first Victoria Line train, as it is about to leave Walthamstow Central station on Sunday, 1 September 1968, while Stationmaster Edwin Austin looks on.

Victoria Line trains in the Northumberland Park depot.

A Victoria Line train passing through the washing plant at Northumberland Park depot.

The nerve centre of the Victoria Line. The Cobourg Street control room with its illuminated panels and television monitor screens.

Opening the Brixton extension: Princess Alexandra, with Sir Richard Way, Chairman of London Transport, on her right and the Vauxhall/Pimlico stationmaster, Mr. C. F. Metcalf, on her left, transferring from northbound to southbound trains at the partially-completed Pimlico station on 23 July 1971.

passengers on the Victoria Line, rattling down an echo-
ing tube tunnel astride temporary seats fixed up on a
contractor's spoil train.

Work, the journalists were told, was going on at 33
sites between Victoria and Walthamstow. The contracts
let so far totalled nearly £23 million, including civil
engineering; 26 shields of various types for driving the
running and station tunnels; and the concrete and iron
segments for lining the tunnels. A problem facing the
builders at that time was the shortage of skilled soft-
tunnel workers. 'In the conditions of over-full employment that exist in London', London Transport explained, 'and with the intense competition for workers
in the civil engineering industry generally, our contractors are finding that it is taking them a long time to
build up and stabilize an efficient labour force of the
size required for this highly specialized work.' The
theme of the need to build up and stabilize—and give
steady employment to—a skilled band of tunnel designers and builders was one which London Transport
was to repeat with more emphasis as time went on.

The Press visit was organized like a military operation.
As everyone had to go down a 72-ft. shaft in the small
cage of a hoist, it would have been useless to ask
them all to arrive at the same time. Everyone was given
a time at which to arrive, arranged so that evening
papers with an edition to catch had priority, the daily
newspapers next, and so on, finishing up with the
technical writers who wanted not only to look but to ask
how and why, and would therefore need more time.
Special arrangements had already been made for news-
reels and television, who had a visit of their own beforehand on the understanding that their material would not
be released until everyone had been below.

Once down the shaft at Cavendish Square, there was
a walk of 100yds. to the northbound station tunnel,
where a 60-ton, £17,000 shield was seen at work extending
the tunnel. Contractor's narrow-gauge trains were
seen hauling away some of the 225 tons of clay taken
out every 24 hours from this tunnel to be carried away

E

by lorries, mainly to be used to fill old disused gravel pits in the Home Counties. In this one station alone, 21 different faces were opened up as the work went on.

Back on the surface, the journalists, still in their small groups, each with its engineer guide, were whisked away from Cavendish Square to the Green Park site, where room had been found for a marquee, for refreshments and a chance to ask more questions.

Fifteen months later the Press came back to this site and went down to the workings. Before, they had seen the beginning; now the work was well advanced. Of special note was the spoil disposal equipment, designed by W. G. Allen & Sons (Tipton) Ltd. to the requirements of John Mowlem & Co. Ltd., the contractors for this site. It consisted of two large steel wagons, or cars, each with a conveyor belt at floor level, forming a sliding floor, and provided with another conveyor belt which would reach between the cars. Each car held 15 tons of clay spoil, or the amount taken out for each 2-ft. tunnel-lining ring. The car nearest the shield remained in position behind the shield and took the spoil as it was carried to it by conveyor belt from the face. This was the 'bunker' car. When the cutting cycle stopped, and the bunker car was full, its load of clay was carried by its built-in conveyor and the connecting conveyor to the second car. This car—the 'shuttle' car—was self-propelled by batteries. Once full, it ran back over a narrow-gauge track to the shaft and discharged its load, using its internal conveyor, on to another conveyor belt which carried the clay to a bucket elevator. This in turn took the clay up the shaft and discharged it on to a tip from which lorries later took it away. On its return trip to the face, the shuttle car carried the segments to make up the next lining ring. Travelling on the slippery floor of this car, wearing bright yellow helmets, the Press were able to ride to the working face and watch the near-miracle of the measuring rods sliding slowly along the newly exposed clay of the tunnel wall as the drum-digger cut its way steadily forward. By now—27 July 1965—about half of the civil engineering work had been completed and 13 out of the 25 miles of tunnelling were finished.

Shortly afterwards, in October 1965, H. G. Follenfant succeeded C. E. Dunton, who had retired, as Chief Civil Engineer. Mr. Follenfant, as New Works Engineer, had been responsible for the coordination of the detailed planning for the Victoria Line and the commencement of construction. He had been Deputy Chief Civil Engineer since 1964.

By April 1966, 20 miles of running tunnels had been driven and on Tuesday, 20th September 1966, London Transport was able to announce that the mechanical digging of the Victoria Line tunnels had been finished that day, when the shield driving the southbound tunnel from Highbury had broken through, 100yds. east of King's Cross, at 09 40 into an already completed tunnel 50ft. below Northdown Street. Only three short sections of tunnel, at Oxford Circus, Highbury, and Finsbury Park, remained to be excavated by powered hand tools. Half a million cubic yards of earth had been taken from the running tunnels and some 300,000 cu.yds. from the various station works—a very small amount for an Underground line of this importance.

IX Engineering extraordinary

THE BUILDING of any underground railway is in itself engineering extraordinary, but the Victoria Line had some special problems waiting, apart from the basements of Peter Robinson's store, already described, and the Oxford Circus 'umbrella'.

At Euston, as mentioned earlier, the tunnels project below the London clay into the less stable Woolwich and Reading beds. When the original Northern Line tunnels were built here the work had to be done under compressed air. This system was also required for some of the Victoria Line work. The principle is that two airtight concrete bulkheads are built a short distance apart in the tunnel and provided with airtight doors to seal off the working end of the tunnel. Air is then pumped into the sealed end until it reaches a pressure which is just sufficient to keep the water in the surrounding layer from coming into the tunnel. Men and materials enter through the outer doors into the space between bulkheads—the 'air lock'. They stay there while the air pressure is brought up to the pressure inside the new tunnel, when the inner doors are opened and they can go through into the workings. The same applies in reverse, when men wait in the air lock for the pressure to be gradually lowered. There are special precautions to prevent both doors being opened at once, otherwise instant decompression would produce the 'bends', the forming of bubbles in the blood experienced by divers brought up too quickly. Materials need not be treated so gently and the opening of the bulkhead door on the atmospheric side sometimes produces an instant fog of water vapour as the air is decompressed. The delay to the work caused by the need for everything to pass through an air lock can, of course, be very considerable.

There are other ways of dealing with loose or water-bearing soil, and one of these was used at Victoria, where the main-line station is built on the site of a former canal basin. Although the Victoria Line tunnels themselves are generally in good clay in this area and clear of the basin, the various shafts down to the new station, including those for the escalators, had to pass through a deep layer of water-bearing sand and gravel. Here it was decided that the ground should be consolidated with chemicals and work began from open-air sites and from below. Soon, however, it became necessary to carry on the work actually inside the Southern Region main-line station, in an area 350ft. long running obliquely under main-line platforms 4–7. Below this area a large-diameter crossover tunnel had to be built with only 7 or 8ft. of clay between its roof and the gravel deposits.

Three thousand 1½-in. pipes were driven 35ft. into the ground by pneumatic hammers and chemicals were injected until a firm layer of consolidated gravel, 5ft. thick and as hard as concrete, was formed as a protection under which the new crossover tunnel could be driven.

At Tottenham Hale an unusual but effective method was adopted of consolidating the loose ground so that an escalator shaft could be driven through it. The ground was frozen. Tubes, called 'probes', were driven down, 5ft. apart, into the ground until they were just above the level of the top of the new escalator shaft—or the place where the shaft would be. As the shaft would slope, the depth of the probes gradually increased from 6ft. to 35ft. The probes were really two tubes, one inside the other, and once in place liquid nitrogen at −196°C. (or 352°F. below freezing point) was passed down the inner tube of the first probe. It rose up again through the annular space between the tubes and was passed from there to the next probe. Each 'charge' passed through about five probes before the temperature rose too high to be really useful and the nitrogen was allowed to escape—as a gas—into the atmosphere.

The freezing process was checked by remote reading of the temperature in small tubes driven between the probes, and as soon as it became clear that an area was completely frozen the circulation of nitrogen was stopped and replaced by brine at $-18°C$. ($0°F$.) to keep the ground frozen. The nitrogen enabled the ground to be frozen much faster than if brine alone had been used, achieving in one hour what would otherwise have taken a day. The first freezing was done round the outside of the area and the freeze gradually moved towards the centre until 500 cu.yd. of soil were frozen. The process took three months, including the hottest part of the 1966 summer. In all, about 270 million B.T.U. were extracted, leaving a frozen area through which the escalator shaft could be driven without fear of collapsing soil.

No matter how carefully the ground is sounded out beforehand, or how many trial boreholes are made to discover the nature of the soil, there can always be gaps where the unexpected happens. Thus unsuspected loose material twice caved in on shields building the new Victoria Line, once almost directly under the bandstand in Green Park, and once in the Lea Valley out at Tottenham. These incidents were soon overcome and served to show, by their rarity, the skill that had gone into the meticulous planning of the civil engineering work.

Another task calling for meticulous planning was the building and, particularly, the connection to the existing Piccadilly Line of the diversion tunnel which would enable passengers to interchange between Victoria and Piccadilly Line trains by walking through very short connecting passageways, at the same level, to the adjoining platforms at Finsbury Park.

Finsbury Park station originally accommodated the Piccadilly Line and Great Northern & City Line tracks in two adjacent pairs of station tunnels. The Great Northern & City (now the Highbury branch of the Northern Line) platforms were opened in 1904 and the Piccadilly platforms in 1906. It was the terminal station for both lines until 1932, when the Piccadilly Line was extended to Arnos Grove.

The Victoria Line same-level interchange with the Piccadilly Line has been provided by withdrawing the Highbury branch service between Drayton Park and

Finsbury Park and diverting the westbound Piccadilly Line to the westerly of the two platforms previously occupied by the Highbury branch. This allowed the northbound running tunnel of the Victoria Line, both north and south of the station, to be connected with the tunnel originally occupied by the westbound Piccadilly Line. The southbound Victoria Line tunnel was connected to the easterly of the Highbury branch tunnels at the north end of the station and occupies this tunnel to within a quarter of a mile of Drayton Park station, the new terminal of the Highbury branch. (The possibility remained of extending the Highbury branch, which has tunnels large enough to take main-line stock, from Drayton Park to Finsbury Park at high level and of operating a British Rail suburban electrified service from Moorgate and in August 1971 it was announced that this was to be done.)

The contract for the Victoria Line works at Finsbury Park, including the diversion of the Piccadilly Line, was awarded in January 1964. The first stage was the construction of two step-plate junctions, which are formed by gradually enlarging the size of the tunnel rings from those carrying a single track at one end of the junction to large-diameter rings capable of enclosing two tunnel mouths at the other. This was done by encirclement of the existing westbound Piccadilly Line tunnel, without interrupting the service, north and south of the station at the ends of the proposed diversion. The shaft sunk in Finsbury Park in 1960 under the contract for an experimental mile of twin tunnels was re-opened and the site of the north step-plate, which was to taper from 29ft. 6in. to 18ft. 6in. diameter, was approached from the southbound Victoria Line tunnel by a short adit or access passage with a shaft 15ft. 6in. deep at its end. At the base of the shaft a space was formed around the Piccadilly Line tunnel and work began on digging out the clay. Another heading was driven from the southbound tunnel at a point about 100ft. north of the station

NOTE: The geography will be less confusing if it is remembered that the 'eastbound' Piccadilly Line runs almost due north through Finsbury Park, and the 'westbound' line runs due south.

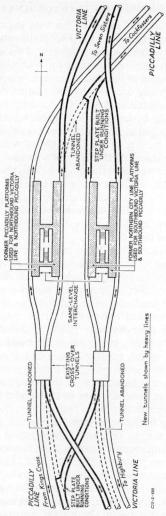

VICTORIA LINE Layout at Finsbury Park station.

to enable the 12ft. 2in. diameter cast-iron lined diversion tunnel to be driven between the station and the step-plate.

Three months later a shaft was sunk at a working site in Isledon Road, south of Finsbury Park station, from which a 10-ft. wide access tunnel was driven under the Eastern Region tracks and both the existing Piccadilly Line tunnels to connect with the lowest point of the diverted westbound Piccadilly tunnel south of Finsbury Park station. The gradients of the diversion were dictated by the need to pass beneath the future northbound Victoria Line and then rise to the level of the existing tunnel before crossing the Northern High Level Sewer between Arsenal station and the step-plate junction south of Finsbury Park station.

The levels of the existing and future westbound Piccadilly Line at the step-plate junction north of the station were nearly equal, but at the one south of the station the existing westbound line was on a falling gradient of 1 in 91 and the diversion track was required to rise at 1 in 90 to meet it, producing a difference in rail level of about 5ft. at the north end of the junction tunnel but almost no difference at the other end. The underside of the existing Piccadilly Line running tunnel was therefore, for most of the length of the step-plate, higher than the level of the future track, and while the encircling tunnels were built the existing tunnel lining had to be supported. Also, the track had to be supported after the original lining had been dismantled. These supports had to be designed so that they could be dismantled quickly when the line was diverted so that the track could be relaid in its new position. The supports were designed as steel trestles, 5ft. apart, with their legs carried on the bottom of the new lining. They were jointed at the surface of the new concrete track base so that the upper part could be removed leaving the centre leg and side supports in place. In the early stages the Piccadilly Line tunnel was supported on timber placed on top of the trestles. At this time, standing in the workings, the old tunnel looked like some monstrous worm threading its way through the new space, except that trains could be seen through gaps, running unconcernedly—if at low speed—through the supported tube.

The step-plates were finished in March 1965 and cable runs from the sides of the existing tunnel were then diverted through the step-plates. This allowed the work of dismantling the old tunnel lining to begin, followed by the removal of the old concrete from between the sleepers. Then the two lowest segments—the 'invert' segments—of the old tunnel lining were removed. All this had to be done at night during the short period —from 01 00 to 04 15—when no trains were running, and the track had to be safe again for the first trains of the day. As the invert segments were removed, the track was supported on heavy timbers which themselves rested on the steel trestles. The speed limit for trains, which had been 25 m.p.h., was reduced to 15 m.p.h. at this stage.

Temporary points were put in at the northern step-plate so that equipment trains could enter and the track could be laid.

Now came the actual changeover, an operation worked out in detail and with great care long before it began. Careful estimates were made of the time needed for each task, a timetable was drawn up, and the work was planned. The key to the whole plan was the use of two overhead runway beams suspended from the roof of the tunnel to lift out the track supports and load them on to works trains. Loading schedules and diagrams were prepared for the flat wagons needed to remove material, every item was numbered, joints were cut in the rails so that track supports could be lifted out as arranged in the programme, and everyone concerned was given a thorough briefing on his particular task. All senior staff were given programmes telling them what had to be done, and when, and who was responsible for seeing that it *was* done. A special service of coaches was arranged to carry Piccadilly Line passengers between Arnos Grove and King's Cross on the day of the changeover to leave the tracks free for the engineers.

Work on the final changeover began when Sunday, 3 October 1965, was three minutes old, and the last passenger train had just passed. A works train, hauled by three battery locomotives, was split into three parts at Manor House (Piccadilly Line) station. One battery locomotive hauling one flat wagon ran to Arsenal station, just south of the new junction, to pick up permanent way materials; the second part—one battery locomotive pushing two flat wagons—was placed on the trestle-supported track in the step-plate. The third part—one battery locomotive pushing one flat wagon—was placed in the new diversion tunnel north of the junction.

The conductor and running rails were removed from the first section of the track and all its supports and equipment were removed and loaded on to the leading wagon of the second part of the train which was then drawn back so that the operation could be repeated for the next section of track on which the train had stood. The first wagon, by then completely loaded, was shunted on to the eastbound Piccadilly Line track at a neighbouring crossover. The other wagon of the second part of the train was then brought back to take the third section of track. This done, this part of the works train was removed, re-coupled to its other wagon and stabled in Finsbury Park station. The flat wagon of the third part of the train was then loaded on the diversion tracks, where it had been placed at the beginning of the work, and taken away.

Meanwhile, 130ft. of track at the Arsenal end was slewed to the new alignment and was supported on special jacks. This left 92ft. of track to be rebuilt, supported on jacks and joined to the 80ft. length of track previously laid. As soon as the old track and its supports were out of the way conductor rails and signalling equipment were installed and the new track was adjusted for running. The signal engineers then took over the whole area, with $2\frac{1}{4}$ hours in which to test and commission the signalling.

With power supply and signal equipment tested and working properly, the junction was handed back to the Operating department at 14 00 and then shortly afterwards the first passenger train came slowly through the new diversion tunnel, over the new track and passed out at the other end of the step-plate on its way to Arsenal station.

Afterwards, at night, the new track was concreted in and the special jacks were taken away.

x The stations

THE TWELVE Victoria Line stations have featured
already in some detail in this narrative because their
basic framework of tunnels was often included in
contracts for running tunnels, etc., but in many cases
other civil engineering contracts followed and, when
these were completed, it was the turn of the architects.
The station work, in fact, and especially the complicated
task at Oxford Circus, dictated the whole pace of construction of the line.

Thus, the second stage of Seven Sisters station—a
£500,000 task—was begun by John Mowlem & Co. Ltd.
in January 1964. An important interchange point
between the new line and the Eastern Region lines from
Enfield Town and Hertford to Liverpool Street, as well
as for bus passengers, Seven Sisters was to have two
ticket halls. They would be built at opposite ends of the
station—one in Tottenham High Road at the corner of
West Green Road, and the other in Seven Sisters Road
near Westerfield Road.

The main ticket hall, 15ft. below street level under the
footpath on the west side of Tottenham High Road,
would be linked by a bank of three escalators to
an intermediate landing 30ft. lower, designed to bridge
the centre of the three Victoria Line tracks. From the
landing, short passages and stairs would lead to the
three platforms.

At the opposite end of the station the ticket hall would
be at street level, alongside the Eastern Region railway
embankment, and the twin escalators would descend
50ft. to another intermediate landing, also bridging
the centre track. Short subways and stairs would lead
to the platforms 10ft. below. A passageway from the
Westerfield Road ticket hall would give interchange
with the Eastern Region lines.

In May came news that work was to begin shortly

on the three-year task of enlarging the Piccadilly Line station at Green Park, intended to become an interchange point with the Victoria Line, and that a contract worth nearly £500,000 had been let to Marples, Ridgway & Partners Ltd. for the civil engineering work. This included extending the existing station ticket hall and making a shaft for three escalators to lead from the ticket hall down to the level of the new Victoria Line platforms 61ft. below. This vital interchange would bring Victoria within the scope of a two-minute Underground trip instead of an eight-minute bus ride or a 15-minute walk for many people working in Mayfair. The ticket hall had to be constructed under temporary decking in Piccadilly, but this was a minor matter compared with the great 'umbrella' at Oxford Circus.

Much more complex was the rebuilding of King's Cross (St. Pancras), announced the following month—a task given to Balfour Beatty & Co. Ltd. at a cost of £1·45 million. Already in four tiers, this station was now to have five, with British Railways Eastern and London Midland Region lines on the surface, the Metropolitan and Circle Lines just below the surface, then the Piccadilly Line, and at the bottom the Northern Line (City branch). Now the Victoria Line had to be squeezed —and there was only just room—between the underside of the century-old Metropolitan Line brick tunnels and the top of the Piccadilly Line tubes. To complicate matters, there are also brickwork tunnels carrying Eastern Region and London Midland Region trains down from the surface to the level of the Metropolitan Line, which has four tracks between King's Cross and Moorgate. The pair of tracks used by the main-line trains have also been there for a century and for most of that time have been known as the 'Widened Lines'. The Metropolitan Line tunnels have no invert—i.e. there is no brick floor—and the inverts of the other two tunnels were never designed for other tunnels to be driven below them.

Rather than undertake the task of strengthening the brick tunnels, which were in use, or underpinning them, it was decided that the Victoria Line station tunnels and

the concourse subway between them should be designed
with linings which could be expanded and would direct
into the ground below the brick tunnel footings most of
the stresses induced, producing little stress below the
weaker parts of the tunnel inverts. Specially strong
tunnelling shields were used for the station tunnels
with extra jacks—33 with a pressure of 25 tons each—to
make sure that the clay face was firmly supported. The
tunnel linings were—like those under Peter Robinson's
store at Oxford Circus—of steel, and they were expanded
against the ground by hydraulic jacks capable of a
thrust of 100 tons each. The whole object of the
operation—successfully carried out—was to maintain
the stress conditions which already existed throughout
the whole of the work so that there would be no de-
formation or settlement of the old tunnels.

The work also included the enlargement of the ticket
hall serving the two existing tube railways to make it
serve three lines, and to build round more than half of
the outside of this larger ticket hall a wide interchange
subway to serve passageways leading to the Eastern
Region King's Cross station, to the London Midland
Region St. Pancras station, to the Pancras Road/Euston
Road corner and to the Metropolitan and Circle Lines
ticket hall as well as both sides of Euston Road. This
subway had to pass through the top of one of the brick
tunnels—the Midland Curve tunnel—and about 70ft.
of the arch of the tunnel had to be demolished and replaced by a flat reinforced concrete roof to make room
for the floor of the subway. The problem was solved by
erecting, in the small clearance between the trains and
the brick arch, a steel shield to keep debris off the tracks.
Demolition was then carried out from above and the new
roof was built section by section.

The Fleet River—or Fleet Sewer as it has now un-
fortunately become—passes close to the ticket hall and
another large sewer passes to the west of the ticket hall
to join the Fleet just to the north. This smaller 4ft. by
2ft. 9in. sewer had to be diverted before the subway
could be built. The roof of the new subway is only 30in.

or so below road level in one section and in this space two water pipes—one 12in. and the other 16in. in diameter—had to be placed, as well as a 36-in. gas main. The 36-in. gas main was of course impossible, so it was converted to two 24-in. mains for a short distance. By partly sinking the pipes in the concrete of the subway roof, and putting steel protective sheets above them, they were squeezed into the small space available.

The ticket hall itself was enlarged to allow the new Victoria Line escalators to emerge into it, as well as those serving the Piccadilly and Northern Lines. This entailed much demolition and placing of temporary supports, for the ground at King's Cross is a filling between underground structures rather than earth with tunnels through it. The whole complex scheme, however, including large-scale ventilation works, was carried out while the station carried its full quota of passengers—amounting to 46 million a year.

The rearrangement of the Finsbury Park tunnels, already mentioned in earlier chapters, caused the Finsbury Park terminus of the Highbury branch, or Northern City Line, to be closed from 4 October 1964. This cutting short of a busy Underground service, essential as it was for future plans, was not undertaken lightly. Special arrangements were made to explain to local authority representatives exactly what was entailed, why the work was being done, and what alternative facilities were available for Northern City passengers.

It was expected that many through passengers to and from the City would continue to King's Cross by Piccadilly or Eastern Region trains and thence into the City by the Northern, Metropolitan or Circle Lines, or travel, again by Eastern Region trains, to Dalston or Broad Street. Still others might find it convenient to use the Northern Line from Highgate or Archway. For those who found it essential to use the Highbury branch, a special coach service, for rail passengers only, was provided between Finsbury Park and Drayton Park, the service being closely tailored to the demand evidenced for it. The coaches were to run for nearly four

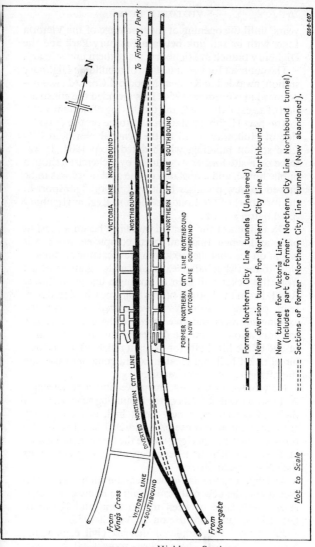

VICTORIA LINE Highbury Station.

Not to Scale

—————— Former Northern City Line tunnels (Unaltered)

■—■—■ New diversion tunnel for Northern City Line Northbound

——————— New tunnel for Victoria Line.
(includes part of Former Northern City Line Northbound tunnel).

= = = = = = Sections of former Northern City Line tunnel (Now abandoned).

FORMER NORTHERN CITY LINE NORTHBOUND
NOW VICTORIA LINE SOUTHBOUND

VICTORIA LINE NORTHBOUND

NORTHBOUND

NORTHERN CITY LINE SOUTHBOUND

To Finsbury Park

N

From King's Cross

DIVERTED NORTHERN CITY LINE

VICTORIA LINE SOUTHBOUND

From Moorgate

C05-6-67

years, until the opening of the first stage of the Victoria Line, with its rail link between Finsbury Park and the Highbury branch at Highbury, made them unnecessary.

The contract for the first stage of rebuilding Highbury station, awarded to Kinnear Moodie & Co. Ltd., was announced in November 1964. This included the construction of an escalator shaft and the driving of twin subways.

The new Highbury station was to be on the opposite side of Holloway Road to the original Northern City Line station building, which dated from 1904. It was to be on a site formerly occupied by a chemist's shop, a public house, and a post office. The post office was to be moved to new premises built by London Transport in the forecourt of the London Midland Region Highbury & Islington station.

Demolition of the vacated buildings began almost at once and when this had been completed work was begun on the chamber to house the escalator machinery close to the ticket hall. Next the escalator shaft was sunk from the ticket hall area at an angle under Holloway Road. From the bottom of this shaft, nearly 40ft. down, twin passenger subways were driven to meet the existing subways and give access to the platforms. The contract also covered the deepening and reconstruction of one of the lift shafts for draught relief, after the combined ticket hall and escalators had come into use and the lifts were no longer required.

Now the work on the stations moved into another stage. At Euston the first fruits of the rebuilding scheme, a new flight of escalators, a new ticket hall, and temporary entrances, came into use on 8 March 1965. The escalators—the first two of eight—were the first ever to be used at Euston, which had been dependent entirely on its then 57-year-old lifts.

At Highbury the half-mile diversion tunnel was completed and the new platforms, built to allow easy same-level interchange between the Victoria and Northern City Lines, came into use on 15 August 1965.

Just before this, some of the last civil engineering contracts were let. These, worth some £700,000, were for work on the stations at Walthamstow (Hoe Street) and Blackhorse Road and went to A. Waddington & Son Ltd. At Walthamstow the contract was for a sub-surface concourse, escalator shaft, and various passage-ways and stairways, including those needed to connect with the Eastern Region station above, and at Black-horse Road—a completely new station site for the only non-interchange station on the original section of the Victoria Line—the task included building a lower station concourse, escalator shaft, subways, and a ventilation shaft.

On 11 November 1966 contracts were let for finishing work at Victoria, Euston, and King's Cross. Under the direction of London Transport's Architect, K. J. H. Seymour, the work was to be done at the three stations by Y. J. Lovell (London) Ltd., Higgs & Hill Limited, and Whyatt (Builders) Ltd. respectively. The work involved the erection of walls and partitions to form various rooms, offices and enclosures and the finishing of these rooms, the platforms, escalator shafts, passages, etc. within the shell already provided by the civil engineers. The cost amounted to £875,000.

Similar contracts, worth more than £1·4 million, were announced in March 1967. They were for station finish-ing work at Oxford Circus and Walthamstow (Hoe Street), both let to Robert Hart and Sons Ltd.; Green Park, let to Marshall Andrew and Co. Ltd.; Seven Sisters and Highbury, let to James Carmichael (Con-tractors) Ltd.; and Finsbury Park, to be in the hands of Whyatt (Builders) Ltd.

The only Victoria Line station to have a complete range of new surface buildings, Blackhorse Road, was to be built on a corner site at the junction of Blackhorse and Forest Roads, Walthamstow. By August 1967 the shells of the below-ground platforms, escalator shafts, concourses and subways were already completed and a contract for more than £200,000 had been let to W. H. Streeter Ltd. of Hampton, to include finishing work on those sections as well as the construction of the surface buildings.

The new Blackhorse Road station was to have a high steel-framed, flat-roofed ticket hall with interior supporting columns finished in stainless steel. Adjoining lower buildings, also flat-roofed, were to be built for offices, staff rooms, etc. The exterior walls, from floor level, are generally of dark-brown facing bricks, with granite-faced precast concrete panels below, and there are clerestory windows on all sides of the ticket hall.

The whole makes an attractive essay in modern station design.

The main entrance is in Blackhorse Road with a second entrance, reached by a short flight of steps from Forest Road, intended for 'kiss-and-ride' passengers.

A further contract, worth nearly £200,000, was let to W. J. Marston & Son Ltd. of Fulham, for work at Tottenham Hale station adjoining the existing Eastern Region station. There are now escalators between platforms and the ticket hall, steps and a passageway from the ticket hall to the British Rail section, and a short flight of steps to Ferry Lane.

On 15 October 1967, trains on the City branch of the Northern Line were diverted through the new half-mile tunnel to the newly built Platform No. 3 at Euston, from which easy, same-level interchange would eventually be available with the Victoria Line. Three new pairs of escalators, with new subways and below-ground concourses, were brought into use on the same day.

The new platform gave passengers their first view of the décor of a Victoria Line station. The style had been worked out after a year of experiments which included building a series of mock-ups of various designs in a disused station tunnel at Aldwych, 60ft. below the Strand. The general effect is of clean, uncluttered space, with light-grey tiling on the walls and a white melamine-faced canopy or false ceiling which follows the curve of the tunnel roof. Between the top of the tiled platform-side walls and the edge of the canopy is a frieze of Victoria Line blue which carries the station name repeated down the whole length of the platform.

The station names, on the well-known London

Transport bull's-eye sign, are illuminated from behind and there are also recessed display panels with maps and other travel information illuminated by concealed lighting above them. Other recesses contain seats moulded from a hard laminate. Litter bins, too, are recessed into the walls. The platform surfaces are paved, instead of finished in tarmacadam as in the older stations. Lighting—to a higher standard than ever before—is by a row of fluorescent tubes, separated by shorter spacing tubes of similar diameter, running the full length of the platform.

On 7 April 1968, a new temporary combined ticket hall at Highbury station—or Highbury & Islington, to give it its full name—was opened to the public and the escalators were brought into use for passengers for the first time. The 65-year-old Underground ticket hall at the station was closed and the lifts were taken out of service on the same day.

Elsewhere along the line the other stations were rapidly approaching completion in readiness for the opening of the first section of the line in September. All stations except Finsbury Park, where the platforms are comparatively near street level, were designed to have escalator connections between the ticket hall and the trains, or for interchange, and 42 escalators were being installed. All except one—the interchange escalator at Warren Street—were designed to operate on alternating current, the first time Underground escalators had been driven by a.c. instead of d.c. on a large scale.

All the escalators have aluminium finishing and treads, and all are reversible. They normally travel at 125ft. per minute, but are capable of speeding up to 145ft. per minute, the speed at which, London Transport studies have shown, escalators can carry the maximum number of people.

Fifteen of them are fitted with 'Speed-ray' photo-electric control to reduce the speed of ascending escalators when they are not carrying passengers. These escalators normally run at half speed at these times, reducing wear and current consumption, but automatically accelerate, very smoothly, to full speed when a light-ray directed on a light-sensitive cell is broken by a passenger boarding the escalator. When the passenger reaches the top (and provided that no other passenger has broken the ray) the escalator slows down again to half speed. The system has been in successful use for some years at selected Underground stations where off-peak traffic is light and intermittent. A new design of drive for the moving handrails ensures that their speed is synchronized with that of the steps.

The new escalators, like others on the Underground, are fitted with safety devices which will stop the machine should a fault develop, and emergency stop switches are provided at the top and bottom landings.

Among the special equipment items on Victoria Line stations are television cameras and monitor screens (of which more later); public information points like those tried out at Holborn; microphones and loudspeakers for announcements and messages, as well as telephones for staff communications; and plungers to stop the trains in emergency.

Some stations also have equipment to make automatic pre-recorded announcements over the loudspeakers.

A pleasant decision was that to have a special motif incorporated in the tiling at each station to identify it easily to regular travellers. All of them have some relationship to the area above, some obvious, some not.

At Walthamstow Central a William Morris pattern reminds passengers that this pioneer of industrial design lived and worked in the area. Blackhorse Road has a black horse and Tottenham Hale a ferry boat as a reminder of the former Lea ferry. At Seven Sisters there are seven trees – a local legend – and at Finsbury Park duelling pistols. Highbury has a mediaeval castle, King's Cross a cross of five crowns, Euston the famous Doric Arch. and Warren Street a visual pun represented by a maze. Oxford Circus has an abstract pattern in colours representing the meeting of the Victoria, Central and Bakerloo lines; Green Park trees, and Victoria a cameo-like portrait of Queen Victoria herself.

XI The trains

IN THE EARLY PLANNING STAGES, an articulated type of rolling stock was considered for the Victoria Line. This means that a set of four cars would have had only five bogies instead of eight, as the ends of adjacent cars would have been carried on a bogie common to both cars. This idea—once well known in main-line practice, especially on the former London & North Eastern Railway—saves the cost of bogies, concentrates the weight to give the motored wheels a better grip on the rails both for driving and braking, enables cars to be coupled closer together, and, some authorities consider, gives better riding. Although suitable articulated trains capable of running over other existing lines to reach Acton Works for heavy overhaul might have been built, there was not sufficient time to develop a satisfactory arrangement within the civil engineering limitations and the idea had therefore to be dropped.

As it happens, a new type of stock had been designed for the replacement of the older Central Line stock and twelve of these cars, all motor cars, had been put in hand before a series of events made it impossible to wait for the new cars to be thoroughly tested before placing a bulk order for the Central Line. As the new Piccadilly Line cars were performing excellently, this type was ordered for the Central Line.

The twelve motor cars (known as the 1960 stock) were not wasted. In many ways they acted as prototypes for the Victoria Line trains, which have a number of their features. Still more, they acted, while earning their keep in revenue service, as the test beds for the automatic driving equipment which was to be the most important single feature of the Victoria Line trains.

London Transport's first automatically operated train, a set of District Line cars, began trials on a one-mile stretch of track between South Ealing and Acton

Town towards the end of 1962. The system used was
devised by London Transport engineers and proved
successful—so much so that the train could be displayed
confidently to the Press towards the end of March 1963,
and on 8 April the equipment was brought into use on
a train in public service. The eastbound track between
Stamford Brook and Ravenscourt Park was fitted with
the necessary equipment, and the train-borne part of
the apparatus was installed in a District Line train.
On the first eastwards run of Train No. 123 that morning, the guard closed the doors at Stamford Brook and
the motorman cut in the automatic control switch for
the first time and pressed the starting button. Then he
sat back while the train accelerated, cut off power to
its motors and coasted, and then applied its brakes to
stop in the proper position at Ravenscourt Park. All
unknowingly, London Transport's first automatically
driven paying passengers had completed their first
trip.

The time arrived when it was essential that orders
should be placed for the Victoria Line trains if they
were to be delivered, tested, and their operators taught
to handle them before the line opened for traffic—yet
the automatic driving equipment was still only in the
test stage. On 10 March 1964 London Transport
announced that a £2·25 million contract had been placed
with Metropolitan-Cammell Carriage & Wagon Co.
Ltd. of Saltley, Birmingham, for the bodies and bogies
of the 244 tube cars needed, equally divided between
motor cars and trailers. Further contracts for the
motors, doors, and all the other equipment were to be
placed later. At this stage details of design and of the
appearance of the new trains were still being studied
jointly by London Transport's Chief Mechanical Engineer (Railways), the contractors, and the London
Transport Design Panel. The dilemma of automatic
driving was overcome by a decision to make provision
in the design for automatic driving equipment to be incorporated should the experiments then being conducted
prove successful.

Less than a month later, on Sunday, 5 April, full-scale trials of automatically driven trains began on the four-mile section of the Central Line between Woodford and Hainault. Four Central Line trains were converted for automatic operation over this section, which includes intermediate stations at Roding Valley, Chigwell, and Grange Hill.

Each of the four trains which were used for the trials consisted of two of the 1960 stock motor cars and two older, but refurbished, trailer cars. Three of the trains were indistinguishable, as far as appearance and passenger accommodation were concerned, from those in normal service, but on the fourth train the front section of the driving car at both ends of the train was partitioned off from the rest of the passenger accommodation. In the separate compartments so formed, the train's automatic driving and safety signalling equipment, instead of being concealed beneath seats and underneath the bodies of the cars, was set out on racks and shelves. These compartments were to facilitate observations and tests of the equipment while the train was in operation. The task of equipping the trains, which took several months, was carried out at London Transport's Acton works.

The trains were shown to the Press on the first day of operation, and Anthony Bull, then a Member (later Vice-Chairman) of the London Transport Board, told them that the Board regarded this experiment as a major advance in investigations into the feasibility of automatic trains on the Underground, its object being to try out these trains on a section of line where the full service could be run automatically.

To test a system of this kind, he explained, it was essential that the running of each train should be controlled by automatic equipment which was actuated by the train ahead. Therefore, more than one train was needed for full-scale trials. The Woodford to Hainault shuttle line, being to all intents and purposes a self-contained branch, was suitable for these tests and had been converted for automatic train operation, together with the four trains which would run the service. The full-scale trials would give valuable experience before a decision had to be taken as to whether automatic train operation would be installed on the Victoria Line.

The system, Mr. Bull continued, had been very largely designed by Robert Dell, Chief Signal Engineer to the London Transport Board, in collaboration with A. W. Manser, London Transport's Chief Mechanical Engineer (Railways), and the Westinghouse Brake and Signal Co. Ltd. who had manufactured the equipment to London Transport's requirements. A very great deal of hard work had been done by the staff of the London Transport Signal, Mechanical Engineering and Operating departments and by the staff of the Westinghouse Company to bring the equipment into service without delay, so that the maximum time could be available for operation on the Woodford–Hainault line before the decision on the Victoria Line had to be made.

The Chief Inspecting Officer of Railways for the Ministry of Transport had been kept closely in touch with London Transport developments and, Mr. Bull revealed, he had that morning been carrying out an inspection of the system and had given approval for automatic train operation to be used on the line, in public service, from that afternoon.

A detailed description of the new Victoria Line trains, issued on 31 March 1965, revealed that the decision had been in favour of automatic driving, and on Monday, 12 July the then Minister of Transport, Tom Fraser, inspected the Woodford–Hainault system for himself, travelling with Maurice Holmes, Chairman of London Transport, in the cab of one of the experimental trains and taking over the train operator's work on one section by closing the doors and operating the 'start' buttons.

The first of the trains, brought down from Birmingham to London Transport's Ruislip depot on their own wheels but without motors and other equipment, were completed and tested at Ruislip and Hainault depots and put into trial running on the Woodford–Hainault line, where every set of the new stock was to be rigorously tested before being transferred to Northumberland Park in readiness for the opening of the Victoria Line. Part of the testing consisted of taking over the public service from the experimental trains, so that passengers on this short Essex shuttle service were the first to travel in the new trains.

The Victoria Line trains, within the limits imposed by the small-diameter tunnels in which they have to run, are a considerable advance on earlier stock. The greater distances between stations on the line, easier curves, and automatic operation, together allow the trains to travel at average scheduled speeds 20 per cent higher than trains on other tube lines.

The Victoria Line trains have the 'silver look' also characteristic of the Piccadilly and Central Lines tube cars, with bodies of unpainted lightweight aluminium alloys which reduce weight and keep down running and maintenance costs. Each train has only one man in charge—the train operator—and once the doors are closed and the twin 'start' buttons are pressed, the trains operate automatically, responding to coded impulses transmitted through the track. Other operating features new to standard rolling stock on the Underground include internal loudspeakers for special announcements to passengers by the train operator; carrier wave equipment which enables the train operator to speak to the train regulator at any time—even when the train is on the move—and the regulator to get in touch with any or all of the trains on the line; and short-range inter-train radio which lets the train operator, if necessary, speak to the train behind or ahead of him.

The bright, fluorescently-lit cars are finished internally in light grey, with red leather facings on the moquette seat upholstery, and extensive use is made of plastics, with stainless steel or anodized aluminium metal rails and mouldings.

The cars have wrap-round driving cab windows—a completely new feature; large double-length, double-glazed side windows; higher door windows to enable standing passengers to see station names without stooping; and door screens set back to encourage passengers to stand clear of the doorways. There are longitudinal seats for 36 in the trailer cars, which allows more standing room for the many short-distance passengers who travel on the in-town section of the line, but the conventional arrangement of cross and longitudinal seats for 40 is adopted in the motor cars so that motor and other equipment can be incorporated beneath the seats. (There is equipment of some sort under every seat on these trains—not an inch of space is wasted.) Armrests of a new two-level type tried out experimentally on the Northern Line, which can be shared comfortably by adjacent passengers, are fitted to the seats and illuminated advertisements were provided for the first time on standard Underground rolling stock. The route diagrams are mounted on pull-down ventilators above the windows, so designed that the cars can go through the washing machines daily without water entering through the ventilators even if they are left open.

With these trains, once the train operator closes the doors and presses the twin 'start' buttons, coded impulses from the track cause the train to accelerate, coast, and brake to a halt at the next station, obeying all instructions given on the way, and slowing down or stopping and restarting as required if there is another train ahead or if there is a speed restriction on part of the route. The train operator, stationed in the front cab, can take over and drive manually in the event of any failure of the automatic equipment.

The automatic driving equipment is not complicated in theory and full technical descriptions have been published from time to time, notably in a paper given to the Convention on Automatic Railways held by the Institution of Mechanical Engineers in London on 23–25 September 1964 by Mr. Dell and Mr. Manser. A brief description of the system follows. It can be divided into two basic parts, the first of which corresponds to the signalling system of a normally operated line and is concerned with the safety of the train, and a second part (which the first can over-ride if necessary) which is concerned with the actions normally performed by a driver or motorman operating his controls.

First, then, the 'safety' system. The principle behind this is that a train cannot run unless it is receiving a continuous series of coded impulses transmitted through the running rails. If no code is received the train cannot start, or, if it is running when the impulses cease, the brakes will be applied and the train will stop. There are several different codes which permit the ranges of speeds within which the train can run, thus a frequency of 420 pulses a minute allows the train to run without any restriction of speed: a frequency of 270 pulses a minute allows the train to run under power at up to 25 m.p.h., and when it is receiving 180 pulses a minute the train can run at up to 25 m.p.h., provided that power is not being fed to the motors. The codes are received inductively by coils mounted on the front bogie of the first car of the train. A fourth code of 120 pulses a minute is also used but this is in connection with the operation of signalling equipment only and is not picked up by the train.

The three slower codes are generated by timed pendulums and associated electronic equipment. The 420 code is generated entirely electronically. The lines are divided into sections for track circuiting* purposes in the same way as for normal signalling, but the state of the track circuits ahead, showing whether the line is occupied, automatically determines the code to be fed to the track in any section.

The equipment on the train responds only to the correct frequencies, and there is a mechanical governor on the train, driven from a trailer car axle, which checks that the speed restriction under the 270 and 180 codes is being observed and applies the emergency brakes if it is exceeded. The holding of the train just below the

* A track circuit—the basis of all modern signalling—is an electrical circuit running through one rail and back along the other in a section of track isolated from those at each end of it. A train on the line interrupts the circuit and thus shows its presence.

restricted (25 m.p.h.) speed is achieved by an electronic governor which switches on the motors if the speed falls too low (below 21 m.p.h.) and applies braking if the speed rises beyond 23 m.p.h.

So far, except for the electronic governor, we have dealt with the safety signalling system, which, as we have said, over-rides commands related to the driving of the train. These driving commands are given to the train by 'command spots', which are short sections of running rail about 10ft. long through which audio frequency currents are passed. No special insulation of these sections is necessary.

In a typical run between stations the train has to start under power and run under power to a point where it will be able to coast to the next station. As the train nears the station, the brakes have to be applied to bring the cars to a halt in the right place at the platform. When the train operator closes the doors of a Victoria Line train and presses the twin 'start' buttons, the train will be receiving the 420 code—provided the track ahead is clear—and will move off under power. (The code being received is displayed in the cab for the information of the operator.) The train continues to run under power until it reaches the point at which calculations and tests have shown that power should be cut off, and at this point there is a command spot with a 15kc/s. frequency current passing through it. This is recognized by the train-mounted equipment, power is cut off and the train begins to coast. As it approaches the next station it meets the first of a series of command spots with speed-related frequencies, a frequency of 100c/s corresponding to 1 m.p.h. Thus the first spot might dictate a speed of 35 m.p.h. and have a frequency of 3·5kc/s. Other spots follow, each bringing the speed down by, say, 5 m.p.h. The speed reduction needed is calculated automatically by a comparison of the actual speed of the train, in terms of frequencies produced by a train-mounted tachometer generator, with the frequencies received from the track. The brakes are then applied or eased as required until the speed drops to

4 m.p.h. The braking is then 'eased out' to give a smooth stop at the platform. The braking is controlled down to this speed by mercury retarder switches which are able to select any one of three rates of braking as dictated by the closeness of the actual to the required speed. A constant-pressure control is used to apply the brakes at speeds below 4 m.p.h. and this also holds the train while it is standing at a platform.

XII Signalling, control, and power

THE AUTOMATIC DRIVING system was described in the last chapter and it is clear that its provision makes a considerable difference to the type of signalling provided on the Victoria Line compared with an ordinary tube line.

One of the main differences is that there are fewer fixed colour-light signals and there are no train stops —the safety equipment which, on an ordinary Underground line, applies the brakes automatically if a red signal is passed. This particular change is more apparent than real, since on the Victoria Line a signal at danger means no code passing through the rails, and the absence of code causes an immediate brake application—in fact, there is a 'command spot' which causes a normal brake application before the train reaches a signal at danger and this is normally sufficient to stop the train at the signal without an emergency brake application being made. If, when the train passes a predetermined point between the command spot and the signal, it is still travelling too fast to stop at the signal, an emergency brake application is made. Everything in the equipment, of course, is designed on the 'fail-safe' principle, i.e. any failure of apparatus will always be on the side of train safety.

Where there are no junctions on the line, signals at the track side are not really necessary, but some (starting, intermediate, and outer-home) are being provided for the benefit of the train operator in case he has to drive manually at any time. A system of 'moving overlaps', made possible by the coded pulses in the rails, ensures that one train can approach, in complete safety, to within a short distance of another when the first train is accelerating away from a station and the second is slowing down to stop at it. On the assumption used in London Transport signalling calculations that a station stop lasts 30 seconds, one train could follow another on the Victoria Line at a time-interval of only 82 seconds.

As far as possible all signal equipment is in rooms at stations, but where a colour-light signal is installed in the tunnels away from a station all the equipment is housed in special 'location cases' which are fastened in line on the tunnel wall with the signal at one end. To save time on the site for repairs or replacement, all the cases are pre-wired and need only a few on-site connections between them to put them into operation.

At junctions and crossings there is an 'interlocking machine'—a machine which ensures, by mechanical locking devices, that points and signals cannot set up, or show as clear, anything but safe routes for the trains. Interlocking machines are used also in normal Underground signalling so that the safety they give on the Victoria Line is exactly the same as on the Underground in general. In a signalbox, the signalman pushes buttons or pulls levers to tell the interlocking machine what routes to set up, but on the Victoria Line (and at junctions on some other lines) this function is performed by a 'programme machine'. A programme machine is an apparatus which carries within it a plastic roll bearing in punched code form the full particulars of a week's timetable, including Saturday and Sunday services. The roll is arranged so that the machine can read from it the details of which points and signals must be operated for the passage of the next train and pass the necessary orders to the interlocking machine. When that train has gone, the roll 'steps on' one position to bring the particulars for the next train into line. In this way it works through the whole day's timetable and after the last train it runs back automatically to the beginning in readiness for the first train in the morning. On Friday night it does not run back but continues on to bring the weekend timetables at the end of the roll into use. On Sunday nights it runs back the whole way in readiness for Monday morning's first train.

Should trains get out of order, the machine has a

G

limited capacity for 'storing' particulars so that one train can be dealt with before another, or of automatically routeing the next train to come along in accordance with the description of that train. If the timetable and the train description disagree the machine will sound a warning to the regulator in a remote control room and if he takes no action will automatically, after one minute, route the train according to its description.

The control room for the Victoria Line is at Cobourg Street, near Euston. It is a circular room with its walls covered with illuminated diagrams of various types. The Victoria Line signal regulator diagram extends for about a quarter of the way round the room and facing it is a desk for a Train Regulator. Behind him, at an angle, is another desk for the Victoria Line Traffic Controller. Generally speaking, the regulator's job is to watch that the trains are working in accordance with the timetable punched on the programme machines, and to observe the movement of the trains. He is assisted by the lights on his diagram, which reveal the whereabouts of every train on the line and the state of all signals. The controller has the task of seeing that the train service adheres as closely as possible to the timetable from the point of view of passengers' requirements, including those connecting from other lines, and having regard to the availability of staff. Before this type of control room was built the controller worked mainly by telephone and was in touch with stations, train and crew depots, signal boxes, electrical substations, and so on. On the Victoria Line he has many additional facilities.

To the left of the Traffic Controller is another panel —the traction diagram panel—which displays the layout of the current supply system, with substations, switches, etc., and shows which sections of the system are switched on or off. There are also switches which allow the Traffic Controller to disconnect the conductor rails in the tunnels from the traction current supply. Splitting the line into nine sections for current supply purposes makes it possible to detect trains with some types of electrical fault as they pass from section to section. From the panel, the controller can also speak by plug-in telephone to any train operator who makes use of emergency means provided in the tunnel to turn off the traction current.

The rest of the control room is occupied by similar, but more extensive, equipment for the control of the much larger Northern Line.

A green light shows when a programme machine is working normally and referring to the timetable and train description. A yellow light shines when the machine has been switched to deal with each train as it comes along ('first come—first served' working), and a red light when the points and signals at the location concerned are being worked by the regulator by remote control from the control room—all points and signals can be worked in this way in emergency. A flashing green light shows that a machine is working to its set programme without reference to the train description.

A programme machine control panel is built into the regulator's desk, and this can be connected, by pressing code buttons for the site and a particular machine, with any programme machine. When the connections are made, the controller can set up the points and signal an extra train, or cut a train out of the programme, or make any other adjustments to the working of the machine concerned. The programme machines give audible or light warnings of any departures from the set working.

There are various emergency crossovers on the line where trains can be reversed if any disruption of the service should occur. As the regulator will be too busy at such times to act as a remote signalman so that trains can be reversed at these crossovers, their signalling has been made automatic and they can be brought into operation by the regulator, who has only to press the appropriate button in the control room. The crossovers can reverse northbound to southbound, or vice versa, and can reverse all trains or any preset number up to five trains.

On other Underground lines the description of a train

is fed into the signalling system by the signalman or programme machine at the terminus from which the train starts. The description precedes the train automatically from signalbox to signalbox (or the equivalent) down the line until the train reaches its destination. As well as identifying the train to the staff the description is used to operate the train destination signs provided on the platforms for the information of passengers.

On the Victoria Line the method is different, the trains identifying themselves by the Identra system. The train equipment consists of a single coil which reacts with two coils mounted in fixed positions on the track. The coil on the train is capable of being tuned so as to vary the frequency which is produced by the two fixed coils as the train passes them. This variation in turn is recognized as signifying one or other of the possible destinations. The information can then be used in announcing the train at stations and by the programme machines in checking the approaching train against the one predicted by the timetable.

Consideration is being given to another method of identifying trains and keeping a full record of their progress. This is the 'train recorder and number writer'. Each train on the Victoria Line would have its number marked in ordinary numerals on the side, and this would be 'read' by a scanning system and written— again in ordinary numerals—on a chart. The moving chart would be marked with a code of dots giving a time reference and marks showing how long each train spent in each station on the line. The pens would be so spaced that all the marks for one train would appear in a straight line if the train was running to time. Any variation from normal performance could therefore be seen immediately.

The regulator can speak to any train operator (or vice versa) at any time, whether the train concerned is moving or not, by a new carrier wave system. This is a great improvement on former methods when the controller could not get in touch with a train unless the driver had stopped his train and connected equipment on the train to the telephone wires provided at the side of all tunnels. The tunnel telephone system is still available as a standby and still serves to cut off current in an emergency by the simple process of touching the two bare wires together or connecting a telephone handset to the wires.

The Victoria Line controller also has the benefit of television: Peto Scott Ltd. of Weybridge have supplied 74 cameras, 42 monitor sets and distribution equipment. Five years' experience in the use of prototype television equipment at Holborn station amply confirmed its usefulness in helping to control the movement of crowds and to deal with emergency situations, and full advantage of the possibilities of this new aid—also tested by underground systems abroad—has been taken.

At most stations on the new line an operations room, generally at ticket hall level, has been equipped with two 11-in. monitor screens on which the supervisor in charge can select pictures from any of the cameras at his disposal—varying from four at Highbury to eight at Oxford Circus and ten at Euston. A microphone connected to loudspeakers on the platforms enables him to make announcements to passengers as necessary.

Cameras are recessed into the walls at both ends of every station platform and are also sted at strategic points elsewhere in the stations, e.g. at the foot of escalators and in busy interchange concourses. This same system gives the controller also a visual link with all Victoria Line stations. He has two 19-in. monitors at Cobourg Street on which he can see images from a camera on each station platform, so that in the event of a delay to the service he can see the effect of the trouble at a glance. A two-way sound system, linked to the television equipment, enables him to hear local announcements as well as to see what is going on within the range of each camera and to speak to passengers through the platform public address system if required.

Monitor screens for the train operators are sited on each platform near the point where the front of the train stops. These screens show the picture transmitted by the camera mounted at the opposite end of the same platform so that the operator can see what is happening at the rear half of the platform in crowded conditions to help him in closing the doors.

At stations where the Victoria Line gives interchange with other Underground lines, only the Victoria Line sections of the stations are covered by the television equipment at present, but the possibility of extension at busier stations is already being considered.

The main source of power for operating the Victoria Line is London Transport's own generating station at Lots Road, Chelsea, recently modernized at a cost of £12 million. The station has a capacity of 180,000kW —enough power to supply a town the size of Eastbourne—and account was taken in the modernization plans of the extra load which would be imposed by the Victoria Line. There is a second, smaller, London Transport generating station at Greenwich, and this is connected to Lots Road by 22-kV nitrogen-filled cables so that the two generating stations can support each other in case of breakdown or other emergency. This ensures that power will always be available from one or the other to move trains out of the tube or shallow-tunnel sections of the Underground. Standby supplies —and regular supplies for some sections of the Underground—are also available from the Central Electricity Generating Board.

The supply for the Victoria Line is taken by 22-kV cable from Lots Road to a switch house in the Cobourg Street building where the voltage is stepped down to 11kV by three transformers. From Cobourg Street the 11-kV Victoria Line supply is distributed to nine sub-stations, at Northumberland Park, Forest Road, Seven Sisters, Manor House, Drayton Park, Cloudesley Road, Cobourg Street, Dover Street, and Gillingham Street. Manor House already existed as a Piccadilly Line sub-station, but the others are new and Manor House has been re-equipped and modernized. The cables pass to the running tunnels through cable shafts which served as working shafts during construction of the line. In

the substations the 11-kV alternating current is rectified
to direct current and transformed down to 630V at which
it is fed to the track.

The substations, through auxiliary transformers, also
supply current for lighting, escalators, pumps, fans, and
so on, and for signalling. The signalling supplies are
generated by motor-alternator sets in the substations
which produce single-phase current at 600V 125c/s.
The 125c/s was adopted to make certain that no induc-
tive effect from the 50c/s power lines in the tunnel can
produce spurious indications in the signal system.

A compressed air supply is also produced in the substations and is distributed through the tunnels by a
compressed air main. It is used for operating points and
other apparatus, and for the automatic fare collection
equipment we shall be discussing in the next chapter.

The main electrical control room is at Manor House,
where the engineers on watch can monitor the working
of all the Victoria Line substations and operate their
apparatus by remote control if required—part of the
Piccadilly Line power supply system is also controlled
from here.

Although Seven Sisters and Victoria stations get their
lighting, escalator, etc. supplies from neighbouring
substations, as indicated above, the use of a.c. escalators
has made it possible to omit the expensive d.c. supply
cables usually found in the tunnels and to provide
stations with an a.c. supply fed to a transformer room
at the station. There are such rooms—miniature substations—at Walthamstow, Blackhorse Road, Tottenham Hale, Highbury, King's Cross, Euston, Warren
Street, Oxford Street, and Green Park.

Before ending the chapter we must mention that all
train movements in the depot at Northumberland Park
are controlled by a shunter from a control tower. He has
a view over most of the depot and also has an illuminated
panel diagram showing the position of every train.
There are no signals in the depot, but all points are
controlled from the tower console and the shunter can
tell the train operators through the carrier wave system

what he intends to do. If the shunter has any reason to think that his instructions have not been understood properly, he can switch on red lights all over the depot to bring all train movements to a halt.

The shunter's authority for movement extends until the trains are in one of two reception sidings at the entrance to the depot. From here programme machines take over the task and signal the trains away down the branch to join the main line at Seven Sisters. A similar procedure, in reverse, takes place when trains come out of service to enter the depot.

XIII Automatic fare collection

IN MID-MARCH 1963, London Transport let it be known that it was investigating methods of making ticket issuing and collection on the Underground more efficient by the use of electronic techniques. The existing system, it explained, was largely manual, apart from ticket-issuing machines of various types, and as well as involving a considerable amount of clerical work was not fully proof against fraudulent travel.

The advice of data processing experts both in Britain and America was being sought, including that of the Advance Data Systems Corporation of Los Angeles, which had planned schemes for the machine issue and control of rail tickets for an experimental installation on the Long Island Railroad and, later, a permanent installation for the Illinois Central. Any change would have to be tackled in three stages, of which the first, or study stage, was nearly completed. Under it, London Transport had invited representatives of the Advance Data Systems Corporation to visit London to study the feasibility of introducing a system of this kind on the Underground. These representatives had spent four weeks with London Transport and had just returned to the United States to prepare a report for the Board, setting out their recommendations. If the recommendations were acceptable, London Transport would then embark on the second or experimental stage of the plan by installing prototype equipment at one or two Underground stations. If the prototype tests were satisfactory, the third or development stage would follow. This would involve the preparation of specifications of requirements for a complete installation throughout the Underground and in this connection London Transport would make further inquiries both in Great Britain and abroad to find out what type of equipment could best be employed for the whole job.

The statement made it clear that any conversion of the

existing Underground ticket system to new electronic methods would be carried out gradually over a period of several years—it could not be introduced in one operation. If the new system were found to be feasible, and if it could be sufficiently developed in time, then London Transport would hope to install it on the Victoria Line when that line opened in 1968.

The system being studied at that time envisaged that tickets would be bought from machines and then 'read' by electronic barrier equipment. If the tickets were valid, the equipment would allow passengers to pass to the platforms, the whole process taking a second or less. At inward barriers, if passengers presented tickets which were not valid or attempted to pass through without a ticket at all, an electronic device would operate to prevent admission. At exit barriers, similar equipment would 'read' tickets presented and check them for correctness. A passenger would be prevented from leaving if his ticket failed to operate the barrier because, for example, he had travelled farther than the ticket allowed, or it was out of date. He would then be attended to by a member of the staff.

Problems peculiar to the Underground which would have to be overcome before such a system could work effectively, London Transport pointed out, included the wide variety of tickets issued, through journey tickets from British Railways, space limitations at many stations, and the need to maintain movement of passengers through the barriers without delay so as to avoid congestion either in the booking halls or on the platforms or escalators. The statement indicated also that an electronic system of this kind would assist in accounting, auditing, and data collection. It would also make fraudulent travel more difficult.

The first practical experiment began on Sunday, 5 January 1964, when an automatic ticket barrier, fitted with an electronic device for 'reading' tickets presented to it by 'inwards' passengers only, was brought into use for the first time at Stamford Brook on the District Line. The ticket gate was installed in the booking hall and passengers entering the station bought special yellow tickets with code markings from the booking office in the usual way and then inserted them in the gate, which 'read' them before the passenger passed through to the trains. Only single and return tickets were used for this first experiment, and season ticket holders and passengers with other type tickets still passed through the ordinary ticket collector's barrier.

This prototype equipment was of the Board's own design and was expected to give London Transport valuable experience as to the effectiveness of a controlled station entry system of this type. Stamford Brook station was chosen for the first test because its moderate passenger movement and booking hall layout made it suitable.

The automatic gate was waist-high and stood next to the ticket collector's box. It had a metal frame, encased in leather-covered soft foam rubber, and was placed between two light grey plastic barrier 'walls' which were slightly higher. The right-hand wall housed the ticket slot as well as the electronic detector mechanism, and the left-hand wall had metal rollers on the top for easy movement of luggage.

A passenger placed his ticket in the slot as he entered the gate, and it was then drawn into the electronic detector, 'read' by it, and returned. A 'Go' sign was then illuminated (provided the ticket was valid) and the gate mechanism was released to allow the passenger through. An invalid ticket was returned to the passenger, but a 'Stop' sign then appeared and the gate would not open.

Warning that these were early days and there were many difficulties to be overcome, a spokesman for London Transport revealed the possibility at some future date of a 'stored fare' ticket for which a passenger could pay a lump sum and which he could then use for journeys on any part of the Underground until the amount of travel represented by the cost of the ticket had all been cancelled by electronic barrier control. This remains, at present, a long-term project.

Just over two months later, on Sunday, 15 March 1964, a further stage in the experiment began at Chiswick Park (District Line) when London Transport brought into operation an automatic ticket gate of different design. This was the second automatic gate to be tried out under normal working conditions in London and was designed and built by the Advance Data Systems Corporation.

The London Transport-designed gate at Stamford Brook and this American-designed one at Chiswick Park were the first in the world to 'read' railway passengers' tickets. Automatic gates had been used on some overseas railways before, but they depended on the use of a token or coin for a single fixed fare, whereas the new system being developed for London was aimed at providing a flexible scheme to cover a wide range of journeys and ticket values.

The Chiswick Park gate—known as the 'Four Door Gate'—derived its name from its construction. It had two sets of double doors spaced a short distance apart between grey metal 'walls' about 40in. high. A passenger entering the gate placed his ticket in a slot in the right-hand wall and it was drawn into the electronic detector, 'read', and returned from another slot on top of the wall. A valid ticket automatically opened the first set of doors to allow the passenger into the centre section. As the passenger entered he interrupted a light beam, or stepped on a pressure pad, either movement causing the first set of doors to close behind him and, at the same time, the second set of doors to open in front of him to allow him through. The second set of doors closed immediately the passenger had passed through another light beam or stepped on another pressure pad. No pressure was needed on the power-operated doors, which opened automatically and as quickly as the passenger moved. With a non-valid ticket, the doors remained closed and passengers were directed to the station staff for assistance.

An important feature of the new gate was its ability to store information. Up to three tickets could be inserted in rapid succession and the gate would allow the correct number of people through before it closed. If successive passengers placed their tickets in the slot rapidly enough both sets of doors remained open and the gate kept count of how many tickets had been inserted and how many passengers had passed through. When the last passenger was through the doors would close. This meant that at the busiest times there would be a minimum of door movement and hence a minimum of delay to passengers. Different arrangements of door operation could be set by simple adjustments of the electronic mechanism.

Only single 'inwards' and return tickets were used for the experiment and these were again coloured yellow and coded with special ink.

A third type of automatic ticket gate came into operation—again for 'inwards' passengers only—at Ravenscourt Park District Line station in mid-April. This gate differed in mechanical design from the two already working at Stamford Brook and Chiswick Park stations but had the same feature of being able to 'read' tickets presented to it by passengers. Called the 'tripod' gate, it had three bars arranged in milkstool-leg pattern angled across the space between its two 39-in. high walls. In the closed state one of the bars lay horizontally across the gap and the other two were placed out of the way. A valid ticket presented to the gate released the gate mechanism. Light pressure by the passenger against the bar then rotated it away and allowed him through to the trains while a second bar automatically came into position behind the passenger to close the gate again. The mechanical part of the 'tripod' gate was of a type widely used on overseas urban railways where, however, it is operated by coins or tokens; it is also used at entrances to exhibitions and entertainment centres, etc. in this country and abroad. London Transport at this time invited the comments of the travelling public on all three types of automatic ticket gate which had now been installed.

The three types of gate, of which the four-door and

'milkstool' type were to emerge for use on the Victoria Line, were now all in use, but all for inwards passengers only, which meant that they had to recognize only one code—that for their own station.

It was on Monday, 17 May 1965, that the first 'outward' gate came into operation. This was at Acton Town station on the District and Piccadilly Lines. This gate could 'read' the yellow tickets issued from about 20 Underground stations for journeys to Acton, the tickets being again specially coded and marked with magnetic ink. Another new feature of this Acton experiment was the gate's ability to handle weekly season and off-peak cheap tickets as well as ordinary single and return tickets. Weekly seasons issued at Acton Town station were of a special size, yellow in colour and with coded markings. The off-peak day tickets were coloured pink and also had special markings.

The tickets used in these first experiments were ordinary card tickets marked with code bars in magnetic ink, but they proved too liable to damage during a journey and not to be sufficiently amenable to close-tolerance work. As a new stage in the experiments, therefore, London Transport changed over to tickets —still coloured yellow—one side of which was coated with a brown magnetic oxide, like a recording tape, which could be electronically encoded at the moment of sale.

These tickets, issued by something like 45 different stations, were used to operate a new outwards gate at Turnham Green—again on the District Line. These experimental gates were all installed at stations on the District Line in west London because they were near the London Transport signal shops in West Kensington where the equipment was being assembled and tested. Also, the installation of gates at stations near each other made maintenance easier to arrange.

Automatic fare collection is not only a question of the recognition of tickets as valid, however, but also in-cludes their automatic sale. The London Underground has for many years had relatively simple machines which sell tickets and give change, but something more complicated was needed to deal with tickets for the new system, since they have to be properly coded before issue. If full use was to be made of the possibilities of machine sales, it was also necessary to have some method of accepting, or failing that of changing, banknotes of the most common denominations.

Hammersmith, used by 22 million passengers a year and where there is a large ticket hall, was chosen as the station where all aspects of automatic fare collection would be brought together, and on 20 May 1966 the first of the new machines, a twin note-changing machine which would give change in florins for 10s. or £1 notes, was brought into use. It was designed jointly by London Transport and its American consultants and was mounted in the wall of a new-style ticket office which opened on 20 July. The new office was designed as a focal point of the fare collection system, the important point being that one window would be on the 'train' side of the automatic gates when installed and the other would be on the 'road' side. The design incorporated two ordinary ticket windows and one season ticket window outside the barrier, and one window inside. This 'train-side' window was provided for excess fare collection, so that anyone who had ridden farther than his ticket allowed—and therefore could not get through the barrier because his ticket was not valid— could pay the excess fare at the window and in return be given a simple ticket which would open the gates and let him out.

The note-changing machine already mentioned was mounted in one wall of the office and a multi-fare ticket issuing machine was mounted in the end wall. This came into use in November 1966.

This machine, capable of issuing tickets for 20 different fares and giving change was designed by London Transport's Chief Signal Engineer's Department to bring within the scope of one machine the issue of tickets for the station's 20 most-used fares. It consisted of two main panels, with 20 push buttons for selected fares from the minimum upwards in the right-hand panel and a comprehensive fares list on the other side. To obtain a ticket from the machine a passenger placed coins in one or both of two slots—one for silver coins and 3d. pieces and the other for pennies—and pressed the appropriate button for the fare required. The machine then issued the ticket and any change due. If the button were pressed before sufficient money was inserted, a figure showing the amount still to pay lit up in a small window and, as further coins were put in, the figure automatically reduced until the fare value was reached and the ticket was issued. The machine incorporated a 'talk-back' loudspeaker so that the passenger could get the advice of the booking office if required. This prototype, from which valuable experience was gained, is being followed by a new type of machine giving similar facilities.

In March 1967 three 'inwards' gates came into use and three 'exit' gates followed in June. In the same month a new-type season ticket which would operate the automatic gates came into use. These yellow plastic tickets are backed with magnetic oxide and encoded by the booking clerk on issue. The ticket issuing machine is of the cash-register type. The booking clerk inserts a pre-printed 'blank' ticket into the machine and indexes the amount of fare paid and the type of ticket, the stations of origin and destination and the route between them, and the date the ticket expires. These particulars are printed on the face of the ticket by the machine. The ticket is then moved on through an encoding section which records full particulars magnetically on the back of the ticket. Ordinary tickets not covered by the multi-fare machine or the greatly improved new types of coin-operated machines—and it is expected that 90 per cent of all tickets will be issued from passenger-operated machines—are issued through cash registers.

Another gate was installed at Alperton (Piccadilly Line) and came into use on 3 December 1967. By now London Transport had had sufficient experience to have been able to order automatic fare equipment for the Victoria Line, and on 12 July 1968 the first four production model gates—of the 'milkstool' type—opened for passenger use at Warren Street (Northern Line), a station to be served also by the Victoria Line a few months later. Warren Street was eventually to have 12 gates, some of them reversible, to deal with all the traffic.

Since then, though not completely ready for the opening of the line, automatic gates of both the four-door and 'milkstool' types have become familiar to all Victoria Line travellers.

The development of these gates has been described, and it will be plain that they act as a strong deterrent to fraudulent travel and reduce staff costs. Eventually the system will be extended until it covers the whole of the Underground.

Although the passenger needs to know no more than has already been said, and his task will be even easier if 'coarsened' fare scales can be introduced to reduce the range of tickets, a short description of the technical matters involved may be of interest.

The magnetically recorded code used for the tickets is the ternary system, and this code is arranged in the form of bars along both edges of the ticket. There must be a bar on one side of the ticket or the other, or on both sides, to give a reading. There is space for 29 marks along one edge of the ticket, allowing for 29 pairs of code bars. There are also extra marks at each end used to indicate which way round the reading head must operate for any particular ticket—the coding is arranged so that a ticket may be inserted in a gate face-up or face-down, and either end first. The actual recording and reading process is very similar to that used in a tape recorder, the code signals being generated by a phonic wheel which rotates with the driving roller used in the ticket printing process. This ensures that variations in speed do not affect the code spacing.

It is not proposed to give full particulars of the code here, but it is divided into sections, each section dealing

H

with a particular type of information. The code allows for many hundreds of possible stations of origin and a similar number of destinations. It also allows routes, dates, price paid for the ticket, type of ticket, and so on to be encoded.

It is not possible to contain all the equipment needed to check the validity of tickets in the gates themselves, so signals are passed from the gates to a 'station calculator'—one such calculator can serve up to 15 gates. This calculator checks the particulars of the ticket against those in its memory store—an immensely complicated procedure because of the tremendous number of variables involved, but performed almost instantaneously.

Regular passengers have shown that they can master the operation of the gates very quickly, but strangers to the system who may get into difficulties through unfamiliarity with the system always have assistance at hand.

xiv Preparing the track

WHEN THE CIVIL ENGINEERING work at the stations was completed they were handed over, as we have seen, to the architect for finishing work—and incidentally to electricians for lighting, mechanical engineers for escalators, signal engineers for public address systems, and so on. The running tunnels remained in the hands of the Chief Civil Engineer who still had much to do—the track had to be laid before any trains could run on the Victoria Line.

The first shipments of sleepers for the line from the Jarrah forests of Western Australia reached Britain in 1964. They were the first of 42,000, worth more than £140,000 and weighing over 3,000 tons.

The sleepers, transhipped to barges in the London docks for the last part of their journey, were taken on the Thames to Charlton where they were stacked at a riverside yard.

Jarrah trees (Eucalyptus Marginate) grow only in Western Australia, and the dark, reddish-brown wood has a hardness and resistance to decay which make it ideal for the underground sections of London's tubes. It remains sound in the dry, constant, warm temperature conditions prevailing in the tube tunnels and needs no application of artificial preservative. All the sleepers and junction timbers in London Transport's tube tunnels are of Jarrah wood and some of the original ones are still in service after more than 60 years of heavy wear.

The work of installing them on the new line began towards the end of the summer of 1964 in the section of 'experimental' tunnel completed in 1961 between Finsbury Park and Netherton Road.

At about the same time orders were announced for new battery locomotives and engineers' wagons for use in equipping the Victoria Line. The locomotive bodies were to be built by the Metropolitan-Cammell Carriage & Wagon Co. Ltd. and much of the equipment, drawn from obsolete rolling stock replaced by new trains on the Piccadilly and Central Lines, was being supplied by London Transport—after attention to some items at Acton Works—for assembly by Metropolitan-Cammell into complete locomotives. The traction control equipment and the large batteries were supplied by the Traction Division of G.E.C. (Engineering) Ltd., the batteries being sub-contracted to the D.P. Battery Co. Ltd. Eight of these new locomotives (there were 13 in all as well as one built by London Transport at Acton) were for service on the Victoria Line.

Thirty-three new wagons—bogie flat wagons and rail wagons and four-wheel hopper and flat wagons—were ordered from British Railways workshops at this time, and, again, many of these were for work on the Victoria Line. Ten of the 20-ton rail wagons were to be formed into two five-wagon rail trains for carrying long welded rails.

The track was to consist of steel bullhead rails weighing 95lb. per yard and welded into 300-ft. lengths. The rails were to be supported on cast-iron chairs which would be screw-spiked to the Jarrah sleepers. The ends of the sleepers would be concreted in and the drainage channel between the rails would be filled with shingle to form a walkway. The accuracy with which the track is laid—and it will be obvious that, once laid, Underground track is indeed permanent—has a great bearing on riding comfort and noise. To achieve perfection in laying the track would entail tremendous costs, but London Transport aims at a very high standard. Welding rails into long lengths also keeps down noise from rail joints.

The first step in assuring accurate track laying came with the fixing of monument plates to the wall of the tunnel at 50-ft. intervals and at every point where the curvature alters. Variations in the position of the tunnels themselves compared with their theoretical line and level (never more than $1\frac{1}{2}$in.) are shown on so-called 'wriggle diagrams' produced by surveying the completed tunnels before equipment began, and the level of the track to be laid was derived from comparison of the 'wriggle diagrams' and accurate marks made on the monument plates.

Chaired sleepers and short, 20ft., service rails were then brought into the tunnels and the sleepers were laid on the shaped invert of the concrete tunnels or the bottom concrete—already in place—in iron-lined tunnels. The rails were then laid in the chairs and an approximate survey made, accurate to $\frac{1}{8}$in. Adjustments were made from this and a second survey was then made of the track to ensure that everything was accurate to $\frac{1}{16}$in. A final survey made sure that, as far as possible, everything was exactly right.

Ready-mixed concrete, sometimes produced in a central plant placed in one of the crossover tunnels, was then brought to the site. Metal surfaces had already been oiled so that the concrete would not adhere to them and specially shaped shuttering was in readiness. The concrete was then poured and compacted into all the spaces round the ends of the sleepers up to the tunnel side and the shuttering, keeping the '4-ft.' way clear, and smoothed to a steel float finish for easy cleaning. Once the concrete had set, the shuttering was taken off for use farther along the line and, since the sleepers were now permanently fixed, the short service rails were also taken up for use elsewhere.

The need for a depot as a base for permanent way and other works trains and a store for materials was solved by using Northumberland Park rolling stock depot, which would not be ready for or receive its passenger trains for some time and where an equipment depot could be maintained even when trains were already running over one or more sections of the line. Here an automated plant with special Swiss equipment was set up temporarily for welding rails into 300-ft. lengths before they were loaded on to the rail trains. Such rails are relatively flexible and, loaded from end to

end of a rake of wagons, will follow the curves of the
track as the train moves along.

As the short service rails had been taken up, the rail
trains had no track on which to run to unload the new
rails, so special skids were made to fasten to the leading
end of each rail. These made it possible for the trains
to unload most of the rails on existing track by pinning
down the ends and backing away from under them, and
then, after the skids were fitted, to push the rails forward
at walking pace until they were lying alongside the
chairs ready to receive them. Then it was only necessary
to lever the rails into the chairs and insert the keys to
hold them. The train could then come forward on to
the new 300-ft. length of track and repeat the process.
Later, conductor rails, signal cables, and so on were all
brought into the tunnel from Northumberland Park
and installed. The works trains took all equipment into
the tunnels at night, leaving them free by day for
installation and finishing work.

The problems of ventilation have been mentioned
before and reference has been made to special ventilation shafts. Heat is produced in the tube tunnels by
electrical apparatus of all kinds, both mounted in trains
and fixed; by brake friction; and by passengers themselves; and all this heat has to be dissipated. The average
temperature of all the other tube lines is 73°F., but the
Victoria Line is designed to keep down to 70°F. Eleven
fans of varying capacities have been installed and they
are capable of giving the equivalent effect of 3½ changes
of air an hour. They are all placed between stations. The
maximum air speed, in the most adverse circumstances
of train movements, is 15 m.p.h. in lower station
passageways and in escalator shafts, and this is reduced
to 10 m.p.h. in station entrances and ticket halls.
Normally, air speeds will be a good deal less.

All the track, signalling equipment, and so on for the
first stage of the Victoria Line—from Walthamstow
Central to Highbury & Islington—was in place, and test
trains had been run in time for the line to be handed
over by the Chief Civil Engineer at 07 00 hrs. on

Monday, 5 August 1968 to F. G. Maxwell, Operating Manager (Railways), for training and test purposes in readiness for opening to public traffic on Sunday, 1 September. The section from Highbury to Warren Street opened on 1 December 1968 and the third section from Warren Street to Victoria was opened by Her Majesty the Queen on 7 March 1969.

The Queen arrived at Green Park station at 11.00, stepping from her car on to a carpet of Victoria Line blue to be greeted by Field Marshal Sir Gerald Templer, Lord Lieutenant of Greater London. Then came the presentation of the Lord Mayor of the City of Westminster, the Chairman of the Greater London Council, and Mr. Richard Marsh, Minister of Transport. The Chairman of London Transport, Mr. (now Sir) Maurice Holmes was presented and he in turn introduced the Vice-Chairman and Members of the Board. After the Board's Chief Officers had been presented, the Queen bought a sixpenny ticket from a machine, passed through the automatic gates, and travelled down the escalators to meet others concerned with the building of the line, its trains, and its equipment.

Waiting below were many distinguished guests from home and overseas. They heard the Queen, speaking from a dais on the platform, recall that in 1890 her great-grandfather, Edward VII, as Prince of Wales, had opened London's first electric Tube railway, and that she and her sister, Princess Margaret, had travelled on the Underground as children. Then she continued:

'I know how difficult, costly and complicated it has been and I know how much trouble has been taken to plan the whole project so that the least possible disturbance has been caused to the public. I am glad that all those who planned, constructed and equipped this line are represented here today, and through their representatives I send my warmest congratulations on the completion of this remarkable work.

'I now have pleasure in declaring the new Victoria Line open.'

Precisely at 11.30 the Queen pressed the twin starting buttons in the cab of a special train decorated with a huge Victoria Line symbol and with the opening date prominently displayed on the buffer beam. Thus began the journey to Oxford Circus—her first Underground journey since the age of 13. There she inspected the station and met others concerned with the Victoria Line. Then she travelled—this time as a passenger—from Oxford Circus to Victoria where she unveiled a commemorative plaque and was presented by the Chairman of London Transport with a specially-bound souvenir book.

At 15.00 the same afternoon the Warren Street–Victoria section of the line was opened for public use and Londoners could travel for the first time direct by Tube from Victoria to Oxford Circus, Euston, King's Cross, Finsbury Park and out to Seven Sisters and Walthamstow.

xv Onward to Brixton

WHEN, UNDER THE TRANSPORT ACT of 1962, the British Transport Commission was abolished and four separate Boards and the Transport Holding Company took over its property and its activities, it was evident that there would still be a need for close liaison in some cases, and in particular between two of them—London Transport and British Railways. One of the main instruments set up for co-operation was the Passenger Transport Committee for London, and this committee set up sub-committees, one of which was the Passenger Transport Planning Committee. This planning committee was charged with preparing a plan for the development and re-arrangement of passenger transport facilities in the London area in the following 25 years.

The Committee produced a report, approved by British Railways and London Transport, in March 1965 and this was made available to Government departments, the Greater London Council, and other planning authorities concerned with commuter travel. The report recommended three new tube projects—the extension of the Aldwych branch to Waterloo; a new railway running roughly north-west to south-east across central London, to be called the Fleet Line and to follow for part of its route the Strand and Fleet Street; and an extension of the Victoria Line to Brixton. This last was no surprise—it echoed the report of the Railway (London Plan) Committee 20 years before—but it showed that the original reasoning had been right and that the need still existed despite the changes brought about in two decades.

Parliamentary powers for the extension were sought in the 1965–66 Session for this southwards extension, which would give a new cross-river route and give relief to both the Northern and Bakerloo Lines. To make the most of the availability of the specialized design team,

I

the labour force, and the equipment brought together for the Victoria Line it was essential that this work (or one of the other schemes) should follow immediately on the completion of the Victoria Line proper. With this in mind, detailed planning was pressed forward and at the end of October 1965 the Ministry of Transport was asked to give its approval in principle, subject to the Parliamentary powers being granted, and on the basis that the cost of the extension should be met from public funds.

In its report for 1966, London Transport was able to record that Parliamentary powers had been granted and that, in March, the Minister of Transport had approved certain preparatory measures including the ordering of segments for lining the tunnels. The report again stressed the importance of an early start on construction to avoid breaking up the Victoria Line team, but at the end of the year Government authorization of the project as a whole was still not forthcoming.

Mrs. Barbara Castle, then Minister of Transport, announced Government approval for the extension, at a cost of £16 million, on 4 August 1967. The 3½-mile extension should be in operation by 1972, stated the Ministry announcement, and was expected to carry 18 million passengers in the first year. As well as having stations at Vauxhall, Stockwell, and Brixton, suggestions from the Westminster City Council, among others, that there should also be a station at Pimlico were to be further examined.

'I have approved this scheme simply and solely because I think it will improve the lot of the travelling public in London,' said Mrs. Castle. 'The new line will bring London Transport relatively little new revenue, because most of the 18 million passengers a year who will be attracted to it already use the Northern or Bakerloo Lines or London Transport buses. It will actually cost the Board money. But, after carefully examining the case for the project against rival calls on our resources, I have decided that the benefit of the line to the public, not least in relieving the congested conditions in which many of them have to travel, will outweigh any accounting loss. So I have given the go-ahead.'

The extension could be the first project on which 'infrastructure grant' would be paid, continued the Ministry announcement. Introduction of these grants, for which the Minister was shortly to seek powers from Parliament, would enable the Government to contribute directly to the cost of building new urban railways and other public transport structures in the same way as it already contributed to the cost of main roads.

As well as the welcome announcement of the approval of the extension itself, the Ministry statement mentioned two points of considerable moment. One was that the project might attract an 'infrastructure grant'. Although grants of this kind, from national, state, or city governments, are common in nearly every country in the world with urban railways, this was the first time that such an offer of help in building an Underground line had ever been made to London Transport. The other point was the reference to the benefit of the line to the public—or social benefit. A social benefit study had in fact been made of the main Victoria Line by C. D. Foster, then Senior Research Fellow in the Economics of Transport, Jesus College, Oxford, and Dr. M. E. Beesley, then Rees Jeffreys Research Fellow in the Economics of Transport, London School of Economics, whose object was to estimate the social benefits and social costs of the line. The study was not commissioned by London Transport but the Board supplied the statistical information required.

Though not the first social benefit study, it was an important one, and similar studies were made of the Brixton extension. They showed that there was a good positive benefit to be achieved by building it.

On the day of the Minister's announcement, London Transport released full particulars of the extension. Among the most telling arguments was that, when the whole Victoria Line was open, the journey from Brixton to Victoria would take eight minutes, Oxford Circus would be only four minutes more away, and a journey from Brixton to King's Cross would take only 18 minutes. There would be a train every two minutes during the busiest periods of the day.

But this was not the end of the Victoria Line story. On 28 June 1968, the Minister of Transport, by then Richard Marsh, approved the proposal to build a station at Pimlico, in the most densely populated area in the United Kingdom, at an estimated cost of £1.4 million.

The decision, Mr. Marsh explained, followed a study by London Transport of the probable effects of a station on the transport situation in the area. This showed that considerable benefits could be expected to accrue to road traffic which would more than offset the small net loss that the station was likely to show in London Transport's revenue account.

Westminster City Council, which had strongly pressed for the building of the station, the statement continued, was consulted throughout the study and the project had also been supported by the Crown Estate Commissioners who had offered to provide, free of charge, easements for the underground workings in view of the benefit to their tenants in the area. The station would be in the neighbourhood of St. George's Square and the project would be eligible for an infrastructure grant from the Ministry under the terms of the Transport Bill then before Parliament. London Transport had been authorized to start work immediately on the platform tunnels, estimated at £500,000, so that the work could be phased in the most economical way with the tunnelling work for the line.

So now the Victoria Line was to have 16 stations and to stretch for 14 miles across London. The 25-year-old plan, if somewhat changed, had at last become reality. With the new automatic equipment—not even developed when the earlier estimates were made—the original line from Walthamstow to Victoria was to cost some £71 million, and the extension to Brixton, with the additional station at Pimlico, about £20 million.

Government approval of the extension came in time to ensure that there could be a certain amount of continuity of employment for some of the highly specialized teams of engineers and other workers who were assembled to build and equip the new line from Walthamstow to Victoria. Some 30 miners were still working on the Victoria Line but it was necessary to build the nucleus up to about 200 to carry out the tunnelling.

From Victoria to the river the tunnels are more than 60 ft. down, but south of the Thames the line is nearer the surface with an average depth of 40–50 ft. Some of the tunnelling shields used between Walthamstow and Victoria were reassembled and used to drive the twin running tunnels and station tunnels of the extension. Concrete or cast-iron segments have been used, according to the nature of the ground, for lining the tunnels. Under the Thames, the roof of the running tunnels is at least 24ft. below the river bed. This section was hand-tunnelled by miners working, as a precaution, in compressed air at 8 p.s.i.

The first sections of twin tunnels driven were those which extend the line from the river towards Victoria and thence under the Thames to Vauxhall, and those between Brixton and Stockwell. The contracts for these sections, worth together more than £4 million, were awarded to Balfour Beatty and Co. Ltd. and A. Waddington & Son Ltd. Balfour Beatty, with the approval of the Minister of Transport, had been carrying out preparatory work since May 1967 at Bessborough Gardens at the south end of Vauxhall Bridge Road to enable tunnelling to start without delay. After assembling the shields below ground at the foot of a 75-ft. shaft they began tunnelling northwards to join up with the end of the main Victoria Line workings at Gillingham Street, Victoria, after which they turned southwards under the river to Vauxhall.

The third section of tunnelling, from Stockwell to Vauxhall, was carried out by Mitchell Bros. Sons & Co. Ltd. The civil engineering work at Vauxhall station, costing well over £1 million, was carried out by Kinnear Moodie & Co. Ltd. and that for Stockwell and Brixton, costing about £2 million, was done by A. Waddington & Son Ltd.

London Transport was authorized by the Minister of Transport to place orders worth more than £700,000 early in 1967 for cast-iron and concrete segments to make a start on the Brixton extension. The orders went to Stanton and Staveley Ltd. for cast-iron segments, and Kinnear Moodie (Concrete) Ltd. for concrete segments, ensuring continuity of production by these firms, who were already engaged on making tunnel lining segments for the Victoria Line. The total value of the complete orders for segments was about £1½ million.

The general method of tunnel construction was the same as that used for the Walthamstow–Victoria section of the line, but there was some bad ground which had to be tunnelled under compressed air. Fifty-seven boreholes were sunk along the route to explore the nature of the ground before work began, revealing water-bearing gravel and unstable clay in the Stockwell and Vauxhall Park areas. There was no run of plain straightforward tunnelling long enough to justify the cost of erecting one of the rotary shields which had been used on the northern section, so Greathead-type shields sheltering miners working with pneumatic spades were used for the whole extension. These shields, in a five-day week, working 24 hours a day, advanced about 150ft. In July 1968 the Duke of Edinburgh and Prince Charles paid the tunnellers a visit and chatted with them deep under Vauxhall Park.

During the tunnelling six fossil nautiloids, undisturbed for more than 50 million years, were uncovered. The nautiloids, a species of large swimming marine mollusc whose descendants are now found only in warm tropical waters, were discovered during the tunnel drive between Victoria and Bessborough Gardens near the north bank of the Thames. They were in separate places at an average depth of 68ft. below ground level, and were identified by a geological expert as the species eutrephoceras regalis.

The Victoria Line nautiloids have now found a new home. They were presented by London Transport to the Natural History Museum, in Cromwell Road, where they now form an important addition to the geological history of London.

Before tunnelling under the Thames began, the geological information already available was supplemented by a seismographic survey carried out from a barge moving across the river—a technique used in North Sea and other prospecting for oil.

The extension which now brings the Brixton housewife to Oxford Circus in only 12 minutes to do her West End shopping made good progress. Except at Pimlico, the civil engineering work was almost completed by mid-1970. The twin tunnels stretched from Victoria all the 3½ miles to Brixton and finishing work was in hand on the interiors of the stations. Track was being laid and equipment being installed all along the line.

The very complicated station construction work at Vauxhall—on the site of the former gas works—is associated with a large-scale road development plan in which the roadway system at Vauxhall Cross is being reconstructed by the Greater London Council. The sub-surface ticket hall, from which escalators lead down to the platforms, was built in two sections, with the Wandsworth Road being diverted over the roof of the first section before the second section and associated subways built by London Transport for the Greater London Council could be completed. The subways give entrances to the station from Bridgefoot and Wandsworth Road, and another gives access to the Southern Region station. The work on the station as a whole involved extensive sheet piling for cofferdams (the Thames is nearby), with a complicated system of ground anchors set in both gravel and clay to support the sheet piles. The ground through which the escalator tunnel was driven was largely water-bearing gravel and it was necessary to freeze the ground in a similar manner to that already described in connection with Tottenham Hale, except that at Vauxhall brine was used as the coolant throughout.

At Stockwell, the existing surface ticket hall of the Northern Line station has been enlarged and an additional escalator has been provided. The new platform layout is designed to give same-level interchange between the Victoria and Northern Lines both northbound and southbound. The southbound platforms are alongside each other and openings have been made to allow passengers to move between the two platforms. Between the northbound platforms, however, there is a lower level concourse served by a new escalator.

Brixton—the new terminus—is of simple plan. Steps lead down from the east side of Brixton Road to a subsurface ticket hall from the other end of which escalators take the passenger down to a low level concourse between the station tunnels. There is a 31-ft. 6-in. wide tunnel containing a high-speed scissors crossover just north of the station so that trains leaving or entering the station can cross to their correct tracks without slackening speed. The 'movable angles' used to give the wheels a continuous path over the crossover are the first to be installed in a tube tunnel. At the other end of the station, siding tunnels run on beyond the platforms to provide space to stable trains overnight in readiness to run the first services in the morning.

The station at Pimlico, expected to open in the autumn of 1972, is also of straightforward design with a sub-surface ticket hall at the corner of Rampayne Street and Bessborough Street. The civil engineering work at that station has been carried out by Balfour Beatty & Co. Ltd. In order to reduce delay in bringing it into use on completion, the station platforms were completed, including lighting, finishing, illuminated signs, platform seats, etc., before the Brixton extension opened. The rest of the work—the ticket hall, the escalators leading down to the lower concourse between the platforms, etc.—is being completed afterwards. Although trains must slow down at Pimlico—as at all temporarily closed Underground stations—they will not stop in the station until it is completed.

Station finishing work at Brixton was undertaken by

Fassnidge Son & Norris Ltd., at Stockwell by Marshall-Andrew & Co. Ltd., at Vauxhall by J. Carmichael (Contractors) Ltd., and at Pimlico the work is in the hands of Y. T. Lovell (London) Ltd.

Pimlico is an example of what was made possible by a significant innovation in organization—project management. In the case of the Brixton extension this meant the appointment of the Chief Civil Engineer as Project Manager and making him responsible for the construction of the extension and the provision of its fixed equipment. He was given authority to oversee the programmes and progress of all departments concerned and to direct the order of works as well as co-ordinate works where there were combined civil engineering and building, etc., contracts. This method of management resulted in a speeding-up of the work generally and at Pimlico made it possible for the finishing work to be started before the completion of construction work and to be properly co-ordinated with it.

The longer line, of course, needed more trains, and the original order for 244 cars for the Victoria–Walthamstow section was accordingly increased by 72 in 1967. The covered siding accommodation at Northumberland Park depot was also extended in readiness for the additional stock. More power is required, and two further electrical substations, a new one at Brixton and a modernized one at Stockwell, have been brought into use to feed current to the extension, and new station transformer rooms have been built at Vauxhall and Brixton. Much equipment of other kinds—including automatic fare collection gates and powerful ventilation fans with a total capacity of 265,000 cubic feet of air a minute—was also provided for the extension.

Apart from giving general relief to traffic congestion on existing road and rail crossings of the Thames, the Brixton extension relieves the peak-hour congestion on sections of the Bakerloo and Northern Lines by giving easy same-level interchange from the south at Stockwell for Victoria, Green Park, and Oxford Circus. Passengers arriving at Waterloo by Southern Region trains are finding more room available on the Underground. It also reduces the volume of interchange at Waterloo by allowing Southern Region passengers to change to the Underground at Vauxhall instead of at Waterloo.

An important, if less obvious, effect of the extension may eventually be to give motorists the chance to park at Brixton and travel direct to Victoria and the West End by Underground, thus relieving the problem of road traffic from inner South London crossing the Thames bridges but this is dependent on local development schemes. Brixton station is in the heart of the area which the London Borough of Lambeth is planning to redevelop as a major shopping and office centre. For motorists it could be a convenient 'park-and-ride' interchange point because the southern section of the Motorway Box is planned to pass through Brixton and at least one radial motorway is likely to join it at or near that point. These developments could increase substantially the number of passengers using the new tube extension.

With new possibilities opened up for them by the new easy same-level interchange at Stockwell, people who use the Northern Line's southern arm to Morden are finding their travel times changed in the same revolutionary manner that had earlier delighted north Londoners. Stockwell to Oxford Circus in 10 minutes, for example, instead of 19, Tooting Broadway to Victoria in 20 minutes instead of 28, are examples of the reductions in time. The Victoria Line is now showing its full capabilities and living up to the standards the planners set for it so many years ago—plans which, where circumstances allowed, have been updated constantly to make sure the Victoria Line has the latest and best equipment that can be devised.

The Victoria Line's southern extension was ready for full train operation—though without passengers—from Monday, 12 July 1971, and for nearly two weeks the trains ran through the tunnels every day, calling at the empty stations where no-one, except the occasional workman or official, could be seen. During this period everything was tested under full working conditions to make sure there would be no failures when the service began. But on the morning of Friday, 23 July, 1971, the trains stopped running. Shortly after 10 30 guests began arriving by road at Brixton station to take up positions in the ticket hall. At 11 10 Princess Alexandra arrived at Brixton to be greeted by Her Majesty's Lieutenant of Greater London, Field Marshal Sir Gerald Templer, who presented civic guests including the Chairman of the Greater London Council and Members of Parliament. He also presented Sir Richard Way, Chairman of London Transport. In a short speech in the booking hall, the Princess praised the work behind the new extension, declaring it a 'very fine example of British ingenuity, industry and skill'. Congratulating the planners, designers and builders, she added, 'Londoners may well hope for similar extensions further afield'.

After pressing a button to start the escalators, she visited the ticket offices and then rode down to the platform to enter the cab of the first passenger-carrying train to leave Brixton. She pressed the starting buttons and then rode in the cab to Pimlico, where she walked through the passageways to the south-bound platform and joined a waiting train to ride back to Brixton—this time as a passenger. At Brixton, she unveiled a tablet by the stairway in the booking hall to commemorate the event. At 15 00 the Victoria Line extension opened its gates to passengers. It was the first section of the Underground to receive a 75% infrastructure grant from the Government, and since the Greater London Council assumed overall responsibility for London Transport on 1 January 1970, the G.L.C. had paid 25 per cent of the remaining construction costs each year.

But should even this be the end? Of the Victoria Line, perhaps, at least for the time being, but an extension of the Hounslow branch of the Piccadilly Line to Heathrow airport is already under construction. The Fleet Line, which would take over the Stanmore branch of the Bakerloo Line and then run from Baker Street to Trafalgar Square/Strand and along the line of the Strand and Fleet Street to Aldwych, Ludgate Circus, Cannon

Street and Fenchurch Street, continuing under the river to Surrey Docks and over the present East London Line to New Cross and Lewisham, is in an advanced state of planning. Parliamentary powers are already available for the greater part of the route—Baker Street to New Cross—and the Greater London Council is paying 25 per cent of the cost of the first section from Baker Street to the Strand with the Government paying the other 75 per cent. Preliminary work on this first section began on 29 September 1971. There are powers, too, for the extension of the Aldwych branch of the Piccadilly Line to Waterloo and possibilities of extending the Bakerloo Line from Elephant & Castle southwards via Camberwell Green to Peckham.

In being, also, is a scheme for a new line which might incorporate the Wimbledon branch of the District Line and cross London via Sloane Square, Victoria, Waterloo, Holborn and Old Street, continuing via Hackney, Leyton and Leytonstone to take over the Hainault branch of the Central Line. There is a specialist team available, with all the necessary equipment, for more tunnelling now that the Brixton extension is completed and they will be used on the Fleet line. Such a team is not easy to get together, but only too easy to disperse.

These extensions to the system are giving London all the benefits of rapid transit railways—now recognized all over the world. Nothing illustrates those benefits better than the record of the first year of the Victoria Line. In the first full year of operation between Walthamstow and Victoria, it carried 70 million passengers, the volume rising steadily from the opening of the line as more people discovered the short cuts and the time saving it offered. The numbers are still increasing. The extra speed of the Victoria Line trains is much appreciated—and is very obvious as one stands on a Victoria Line platform and watches a train come in at a faster rate than on other lines, applying its brakes automatically at exactly the right moment to come to a halt within a very short distance of the stopping mark on the platform edge.

Automatic fare collection has become a part of everyday life to Victoria Line commuters. Just as passengers have become used to the equipment, the equipment itself has improved in performance as snags have been discovered and overcome and the staff have become expert at diagnosing faults and helping passengers to understand the system. The accuracy with which the machines 'read' the encoded tickets—with, of course, the accuracy of encoding which is essential before the tickets can be read at all—is now around 99 per cent, but London Transport will not be satisfied until the figure has reached 99·7 per cent or better.

In general, the multitude of new apparatus being used on a large scale for the first time on the Victoria Line has worked very well indeed and the staff using it have developed a new pride in it. Far from automation and electronics making them more remote from their work, they have brought them closer. The controller and regulator at Cobourg Street no longer depend on telephoned reports on which to make their decisions. The illuminated diagrams and the television monitors let them see for themselves exactly what is happening. The train operator is no longer a lonely man in his cab at the front of the train. He can speak to or receive messages from the control room at any time and speak to his passengers over the public address equipment if the need arises.

The Victoria Line is not just another Underground railway. It is the first of a new generation of such railways, so advanced that London Transport is now giving much thought to what can be done to raise its other lines in due course—finance permitting—to similar standards.

In 1863 London was the first of the world's great cities to have an Underground railway. The reasons for building that first line are just those which make more lines imperative today to keep London on the move.

Printed in Great Britain for the Publicity Office,
London Transport at The Curwen Press, London E13.